The Inspector-General

Nicolai Gogol

Translated by Thomas Seltzer

INTRODUCTION

The Inspector-General is a national institution. To place a purely literary valuation upon it and call it the greatest of Russian comedies would not convey the significance of its position either in Russian literature or in Russian life itself. There is no other single work in the modern literature of any language that carries with it the wealth of associations which the Inspector-General does to the educated Russian. The Germans have their Faust; but Faust is a tragedy with a cosmic philosophic theme. In England it takes nearly all that is implied in the comprehensive name of Shakespeare to give the same sense of bigness that a Russian gets from the mention of the Revizor.

That is not to say that the Russian is so defective in the critical faculty as to balance the combined creative output of the greatest English dramatist against Gogol's one comedy, or even to attribute to it the literary value of any of Shakespeare's better plays. What the Russian's appreciation indicates is the pregnant role that literature plays in the life of intellectual Russia. Here literature is not a luxury, not a diversion. It is bone of the bone, flesh of the flesh, not only of the intelligentsia, but also of a growing number of the common people, intimately woven into their everyday existence, part and parcel of their thoughts, their aspirations, their social, political and economic life. It expresses their collective wrongs and sorrows, their collective hopes and strivings. Not only does it serve to lead the movements of the masses, but it is an integral component element of those movements. In a word, Russian literature is completely bound up with the life of Russian society, and its vitality is but the measure of the spiritual vitality of that society.

This unique character of Russian literature may be said to have had its beginning with the Inspector-General. Before Gogol most Russian writers, with few exceptions, were but weak imitators of foreign models. The drama fashioned itself chiefly upon French patterns. The Inspector-General and later Gogol's novel, Dead Souls, established that tradition in Russian letters which was followed by all the great writers from Dostoyevsky down to Gorky.

As with one blow, Gogol shattered the notions of the theatre-going public of his day of what a comedy should be. The ordinary idea of a play at that time in Russia seems to have been a little like our own tired business man's. And the shock the Revizor gave those early nineteenth-century Russian audiences is not unlike the shocks we ourselves get when once in a while a theatrical manager is courageous enough to produce a bold modern European play. Only the intensity of the shock was much greater. For Gogol dared not only bid defiance to the accepted method; he dared to introduce a subject-matter that under the guise of humor audaciously attacked the very foundation of the state, namely, the officialdom of the Russian bureaucracy. That is why the Revizor marks such a revolution in the world of Russian letters. In form it was realistic, in substance it was vital. It showed up the rottenness and corruption of the instruments through which the Russian government functioned. It held up to ridicule, directly, all the officials of a typical Russian municipality, and, indirectly, pointed to the same system of graft and corruption among the very highest servants of the crown.

What wonder that the Inspector-General became a sort of comedy-epic in the land of the Czars, the land where each petty town-governor is almost an absolute despot, regulating his persecutions and extortions according to the sage saying of the town-governor in the play, "That's the way God made the world, and the Voltairean free-thinkers can talk against it all they like, it won't do any good." Every subordinate in the town administration, all the way down the line to the policemen, follow--not always so scrupulously-- the law laid down by the same authority, "Graft no higher than your rank." As in city and town, so in village and hamlet. It is the tragedy of Russian life, which has its roots in that more comprehensive tragedy, Russian despotism, the despotism that gives the sharp edge to official corruption. For there is no possible redress from it except in violent revolutions.

That is the prime reason why the Inspector-General, a mere comedy, has such a hold on the Russian people and occupies so important a place in Russian literature. And that is why a Russian critic says, "Russia possesses only one comedy, the Inspector-General."

The second reason is the brilliancy and originality with which this national theme was executed. Gogol was above all else the artist. He was not a radical, nor even a liberal. He was strictly conservative. While hating the bureaucracy, yet he never found fault with the system itself or with the autocracy. Like most born artists, he was strongly individualistic in temperament, and his satire and ridicule were aimed not at causes, but at effects. Let but the individuals act morally, and the system, which Gogol never questioned, would work beautifully. This conception caused Gogol to concentrate his best efforts upon delineation of character. It was the characters that were to be revealed, their actions to be held up to scorn and ridicule, not the conditions which created the characters and made them act as they did. If any lesson at all was to be drawn from the play it was not a sociological lesson, but a moral one. The individual who sees himself mirrored in it may be moved to self-purgation; society has nothing to learn from it.

Yet the play lives because of the social message it carries. The creation proved greater than the creator. The author of the Revizor was a poor critic of his own work. The Russian people rejected his estimate and put their own upon it. They knew their officials and they entertained no illusions concerning their regeneration so long as the system that bred them continued to live. Nevertheless, as a keen satire and a striking exposition of the workings of the hated system itself, they hailed the Revizor with delight. And as such it has remained graven in Russia's conscience to this day.

It must be said that "Gogol himself grew with the writing of the Revizor." Always a careful craftsman, scarcely ever satisfied with the first version of a story or a play, continually changing and rewriting, he seems to have bestowed special attention on perfecting this comedy. The subject, like that of Dead Souls, was suggested to him by the poet Pushkin, and was based on a true incident. Pushkin at once recognized Gogol's genius and looked upon the young author as the rising star of Russian literature. Their acquaintance soon ripened into intimate friendship, and Pushkin missed no opportunity to encourage and stimulate him in his writings and help him with all the power of his great influence. Gogol began to work on the play at the close of 1834, when he was twenty-five years old. It was first produced in St. Petersburg, in 1836. Despite the many elaborations it had undergone before Gogol permitted it to be put on the stage, he still did not feel satisfied, and he began to work on it again in 1838. It was not brought down to its present final form until 1842.

Thus the Revizor occupied the mind of the author over a period of eight years, and resulted in a product which from the point of view of characterization and dramatic technique is almost flawless. Yet far more important is the fact that the play marked an epoch in Gogol's own literary development. When he began on it, his ambitions did not rise above making it a comedy of pure fun, but, gradually, in the course of his working on it, the possibilities of the subject unfolded themselves and influenced his entire subsequent career. His art broadened and deepened and grew more serious. If Pushkin's remark, that "behind his laughter you feel the sad tears," is true of some of Gogol's former productions, it is still truer of the Revizor and his later works.

A new life had begun for him, he tells us himself, when he was no longer "moved by childish notions, but by lofty ideas full of truth." "It was Pushkin," he writes, "who made me look at the thing seriously. I saw that in my writings I laughed vainly, for nothing, myself not knowing why. If I was to laugh, then I had better laugh over things that are really to be laughed at. In the Inspector-General I resolved to gather together all the bad in Russia I then knew into one heap, all the injustice that was practised in those places and in those human relations in which more than in anything justice is demanded of men, and to have one big laugh over it all. But that, as is well known, produced an outburst of excitement. Through my laughter, which never before came to me with such force, the reader sensed profound sorrow. I myself felt that my laughter was no longer the same as it had been, that in my writings I could no longer be the same as in the past, and that the need to divert myself with innocent, careless scenes had ended along with my young years."

With the strict censorship that existed in the reign of Czar Nicholas I, it required powerful influence to obtain permission for the production of the comedy. This Gogol received through the instrumentality of his friend, Zhukovsky, who succeeded in gaining the Czar's personal intercession. Nicholas himself was present at the first production in April, 1836, and laughed and applauded, and is said to have remarked, "Everybody gets it, and I most of all."

Naturally official Russia did not relish this innovation in dramatic art, and indignation ran high among them and their supporters. Bulgarin led the attack. Everything that is usually said against a new departure in literature or art was said against the Revizor. It was not original. It was improbable, impossible, coarse, vulgar; lacked plot. It turned on a stale anecdote that everybody knew. It was a rank farce. The characters were mere caricatures. "What sort of a town was it that did not hold a single honest soul?"

Gogol's sensitive nature shrank before the tempest that burst upon him, and he fled from his enemies all the way out of Russia. "Do what you please about presenting the play in Moscow," he writes to Shchepkin four days after its first production in St. Petersburg. "I am not going to bother about it. I am sick of the play and all the fussing over it. It produced a great noisy effect. All are against me . . . they abuse me and go to see it. No tickets can be obtained for the fourth performance."

But the best literary talent of Russia, with Pushkin and Bielinsky, the greatest critic Russia has produced, at the head, ranged itself on his side.

Nicolay Vasilyevich Gogol was born in Sorochintzy, government of Poltava, in 1809. His father was a Little Russian, or Ukrainian, landowner, who exhibited considerable talent as a playwright and actor. Gogol was educated at home until the age of ten, then went to Niezhin, where he entered the gymnasium in 1821. Here he edited a students' manuscript magazine called the Star, and later founded a students' theatre, for which he was both manager and actor. It achieved such success that it was patronized by the general public.

In 1829 Gogol went to St. Petersburg, where he thought of becoming an actor, but he finally gave up the idea and took a position as a subordinate government clerk. His real literary career began in 1830 with the publication of a series of stories of Little Russian country life called Nights on a Farm near Dikanka. In 1831 he became acquainted with Pushkin and Zhukovsky, who introduced the "shy Khokhol" (nickname for "Little Russian"), as he was called, to the house of Madame O. A. Smirnov, the centre of "an intimate circle of literary men and the flower of intellectual society." The same year he obtained a position as instructor of history at the Patriotic Institute, and in 1834 was made professor of history at the University of St. Petersburg. Though his lectures were marked by originality and vivid presentation, he seems on the whole not to have been successful as a professor, and he resigned in 1835.

During this period he kept up his literary activity uninterruptedly, and in 1835 published his collection of stories, Mirgorod, containing How Ivan Ivanovich Quarreled with Ivan Nikiforovich, Taras Bulba, and others. This collection firmly established his position as a leading author. At the same time he was at work on several plays. The Vladimir Cross, which was to deal with the higher St. Petersburg functionaries in the same way as the Revizor with the lesser town officials, was never concluded, as Gogol realized the impossibility of placing them on the Russian stage. A few strong scenes were published. The comedy Marriage, finished in 1835, still finds a place in the Russian theatrical repertoire. The Gamblers, his only other complete comedy, belongs to a later period.

After a stay abroad, chiefly in Italy, lasting with some interruptions for seven years (1836-1841), he returned to his native country, bringing with him the first part of his greatest work, Dead Souls. The novel, published the following year, produced a profound impression and made Gogol's literary reputation supreme. Pushkin, who did not live to see its publication, on hearing the first chapters read, exclaimed, "God, how sad our Russia is!" And Alexander Hertzen characterized it as "a wonderful book, a bitter, but not hopeless rebuke of contemporary Russia." Aksakov went so far as to call it the Russian national epic, and Gogol the Russian Homer.

Unfortunately the novel remained incomplete. Gogol began to suffer from a nervous illness which induced extreme hypochondria. He became excessively religious, fell under the influence of pietists and a fanatical priest, sank more and more into mysticism, and went on a pilgrimage to Jerusalem to worship at the Holy Sepulchre. In this state of mind he came to consider all literature, including his own, as pernicious and sinful.

After burning the manuscript of the second part of Dead Souls, he began to rewrite it, had it completed and ready for the press by 1851, but kept the copy and burned it again a few days before his death (1852), so that it is extant only in parts.

THOMAS SELTZER.

CHARACTERS OF THE PLAY

ANTON ANTONOVICH SKVOZNIK-DMUKHANOVSKY, the Governor. ANNA ANDREYEVNA, his wife. MARYA ANTONOVNA, his daughter. LUKA LUKICH KHLOPOV, the Inspector of Schools. His Wife. AMMOS FIODOROVICH LIAPKIN-TIAPKIN, the Judge. ARTEMY FILIPPOVICH ZEMLIANIKA, the Superintendent of Charities. IVAN KUZMICH SHPEKIN, the Postmaster. PIOTR IVANOVICH DOBCHINSKY. } PIOTR IVANOVICH BOBCHINSKY. } Country Squires. IVAN ALEKSANDROVICH KHLESTAKOV, an official from St. Petersburg. OSIP, his servant. CHRISTIAN IVANOVICH HÜBNER, the district Doctor.

FIODR ANDREYEVICH LIULIUKOV. } ex-officials, }esteemed IVAN LAZAREVICH RASTAKOVSKY. }personages STEPAN IVANOVICH KOROBKIN. }of the town. STEPAN ILYICH UKHOVERTOV, the Police Captain. SVISTUNOV. } PUGOVITZYN. }Police Sergeants. DERZHIMORDA. } ABDULIN, a Merchant. FEVRONYA PETROVA POSHLIOPKINA, the Locksmith's wife. The Widow of a non-commissioned Officer. MISHKA, the Governor's Servant. Servant at the Inn. Guests, Merchants, Citizens, and Petitioners.

CHARACTERS AND COSTUMES

DIRECTIONS FOR ACTORS

THE GOVERNOR.--A man grown old in the service, by no means a fool in his own way. Though he takes bribes, he carries himself with dignity. He is of a rather serious turn and even given somewhat to ratiocination. He speaks in a voice neither too loud nor too low and says neither too much nor too little. Every word of his counts. He has the typical hard stern features of the official who has worked his way up from the lowest rank in the arduous government service. Coarse in his inclinations, he passes rapidly from fear to joy, from servility to arrogance. He is dressed in uniform with frogs and wears Hessian boots with spurs. His hair with a sprinkling of gray is close-cropped.

ANNA ANDREYEVNA.--A provincial coquette, still this side of middle age, educated on novels and albums and on fussing with household affairs and servants. She is highly inquisitive and has streaks of vanity. Sometimes she gets the upper hand over her husband, and he gives in simply because at the moment he cannot find the right thing to say. Her ascendency, however, is confined to mere trifles and takes the form of lecturing and twitting. She changes her dress four times in the course of the play.

KHLESTAKOV.--A skinny young man of about twenty-three, rather stupid, being, as they say, "without a czar in his head," one of those persons called an "empty vessel" in the government offices. He speaks and acts without stopping to think and utterly lacks the power of concentration. The words burst from his mouth unexpectedly. The more naiveté and ingenousness the actor puts into the character the better will he sustain the role. Khlestakov is dressed in the latest fashion.

OSIP.--A typical middle-aged servant, grave in his address, with eyes always a bit lowered. He is argumentative and loves to read sermons directed at his master. His voice is usually monotonous. To his master his tone is blunt and sharp, with even a touch of rudeness. He is the cleverer of the two and grasps a situation more quickly. But he does not like to talk. He is a silent, uncommunicative rascal. He wears a shabby gray or blue coat.

BOBCHINSKY AND DOBCHINSKY.--Short little fellows, strikingly like each other. Both have small paunches, and talk rapidly, with emphatic gestures of their hands, features and bodies. Dobchinsky is slightly the taller and more subdued in manner. Bobchinsky is freer, easier and livelier. They are both exceedingly inquisitive.

LIAPKIN-TIAPKIN.--He has read four or five books and so is a bit of a freethinker. He is always seeing a hidden meaning in things and therefore puts weight into every word he utters. The actor should preserve an expression of importance throughout. He speaks in a bass voice, with a prolonged rattle and wheeze in his throat, like an old-fashioned clock, which buzzes before it strikes.

ZEMLIANIKA.--Very fat, slow and awkward; but for all that a sly, cunning scoundrel. He is very obliging and officious.

SHPEKIN.--Guileless to the point of simplemindedness. The other characters require no special explanation, as their originals can be met almost anywhere.

The actors should pay especial attention to the last scene. The last word uttered must strike all at once, suddenly, like an electric shock. The whole group should change its position at the same instant. The ladies must all burst into a simultaneous cry of astonishment, as if with one throat. The neglect of these directions may ruin the whole effect.

THE INSPECTOR-GENERAL

ACT I

A Room in the Governor's House.

SCENE I

Anton Antonovich, the Governor, Artemy Filippovich, the Superintendent of Charities, Luka Lukich, the Inspector of Schools, Ammos Fiodorovich, the Judge, Stepan Ilyich, Christian Ivanovich, the Doctor, and two Police Sergeants.

GOVERNOR. I have called you together, gentlemen, to tell you an unpleasant piece of news. An Inspector-General is coming.

AMMOS FIOD. What, an Inspector-General?

ARTEMY FIL. What, an Inspector-General?

GOVERNOR. Yes, an Inspector from St. Petersburg, incognito. And with secret instructions, too.

AMMOS. A pretty how-do-you-do!

ARTEMY. As if we hadn't enough trouble without an Inspector!

LUKA LUKICH. Good Lord! With secret instructions!

GOVERNOR. I had a sort of presentiment of it. Last night I kept dreaming of two rats--regular monsters! Upon my word, I never saw the likes of them--black and supernaturally big. They came in, sniffed, and then went away.-- Here's a letter I'll read to you--from Andrey Ivanovich. You know him, Artemy Filippovich. Listen to what he writes: "My dear friend, godfather and benefactor--[He mumbles, glancing rapidly down the page.]--and to let you know"-- Ah, that's it-- "I hasten to let you know, among other things, that an official has arrived here with instructions to inspect the whole government, and your district especially. [Raises his finger significantly.] I have learned of his being here from highly trustworthy sources, though he pretends to be a private person. So, as you have your little peccadilloes, you know, like everybody else--you are a sensible man, and you don't let the good things that come your way slip by-

-" [Stopping] H'm, that's his junk --"I advise you to take precautions, as he may arrive any hour, if he hasn't already, and is not staying somewhere incognito. --Yesterday--" The rest are family matters. "Sister Anna Krillovna is here visiting us with her husband. Ivan Krillovich has grown very fat and is always playing the fiddle"--et cetera, et cetera. So there you have the situation we are confronted with, gentlemen.

AMMOS. An extraordinary situation, most extraordinary! Something behind it, I am sure.

LUKA. But why, Anton Antonovich? What for? Why should we have an Inspector?

GOVERNOR. It's fate, I suppose. [Sighs.] Till now, thank goodness, they have been nosing about in other towns. Now our turn has come.

AMMOS. My opinion is, Anton Antonovich, that the cause is a deep one and rather political in character. It means this, that Russia--yes--that Russia intends to go to war, and the Government has secretly commissioned an official to find out if there is any treasonable activity anywhere.

GOVERNOR. The wise man has hit on the very thing. Treason in this little country town! As if it were on the frontier! Why, you might gallop three years away from here and reach nowhere.

AMMOS. No, you don't catch on--you don't-- The Government is shrewd. It makes no difference that our town is so remote. The Government is on the look-out all the same--

GOVERNOR [cutting him short]. On the look-out, or not on the look-out, anyhow, gentlemen, I have given you warning. I have made some arrangements for myself, and I advise you to do the same. You especially, Artemy Filippovich. This official, no doubt, will want first of all to inspect your department. So you had better see to it that everything is in order, that the night-caps are clean, and the patients don't go about as they usually do, looking as grimy as blacksmiths.

ARTEMY. Oh, that's a small matter. We can get night-caps easily enough.

GOVERNOR. And over each bed you might hang up a placard stating in Latin or some other language--that's your end of it, Christian Ivanovich-- the name of the disease, when the patient fell ill, the day of the week and the month. And I don't like your invalids to be smoking such strong tobacco. It makes you sneeze when you come in. It would be better, too, if there weren't so many of them. If there are a large number, it will instantly be ascribed to bad supervision or incompetent medical treatment.

ARTEMY. Oh, as to treatment, Christian Ivanovich and I have worked out our own system. Our rule is: the nearer to nature the better. We use no expensive medicines. A man is a simple affair. If he dies, he'd die anyway. If he gets well, he'd get well anyway. Besides, the doctor would have a hard time making the patients understand him. He doesn't know a word of Russian.

The Doctor gives forth a sound intermediate between M and A.

GOVERNOR. And you, Ammos Fiodorovich, had better look to the courthouse. The attendants have turned the entrance hall where the petitioners usually wait into a poultry yard, and the geese and goslings go poking their beaks between people's legs. Of course, setting up housekeeping is commendable, and there is no reason why a porter shouldn't do it. Only, you see, the courthouse is not exactly the place for it. I had meant to tell you so before, but somehow it escaped my memory.

AMMOS. Well, I'll have them all taken into the kitchen to-day. Will you come and dine with me?

GOVERNOR. Then, too, it isn't right to have the courtroom littered up with all sorts of rubbish--to have a hunting-crop lying right among the papers on your desk. You're fond of sport, I know, still it's better to have the crop removed for the present. When the Inspector is gone, you may put it back again. As for your assessor, he's an educated man, to be sure, but he reeks of spirits, as if he had just emerged from a distillery. That's not right either. I had meant to tell you so long ago, but something or other drove the thing out of my mind. If his odor is really a congenital defect, as he says, then there are ways of remedying it. You might advise him to eat onion or garlic, or something of the sort. Christian Ivanovich can help him out with some of his nostrums.

The Doctor makes the same sound as before.

AMMOS. No, there's no cure for it. He says his nurse struck him when he was a child, and ever since he has smelt of vodka.

GOVERNOR. Well, I just wanted to call your attention to it. As regards the internal administration and what Andrey Ivanovich in his letter calls "little peccadilloes," I have nothing to say. Why, of course, there isn't a man living who hasn't some sins to answer for. That's the way God made the world, and the Voltairean freethinkers can talk against it all they like, it won't do any good.

AMMOS. What do you mean by sins? Anton Antonovich? There are sins and sins. I tell everyone plainly that I take bribes. I make no bones about it. But what kind of bribes? White greyhound puppies. That's quite a different matter.

GOVERNOR. H'm. Bribes are bribes, whether puppies or anything else.

AMMOS. Oh, no, Anton Antonovich. But if one has a fur overcoat worth five hundred rubles, and one's wife a shawl--

GOVERNOR. [testily]. And supposing greyhound puppies are the only bribes you take? You're an atheist, you never go to church, while I at least am a firm believer and go to church every Sunday. You--oh, I know you. When you begin to talk about the Creation it makes my flesh creep.

AMMOS. Well, it's a conclusion I've reasoned out with my own brain.

GOVERNOR. Too much brain is sometimes worse than none at all.-- However, I merely mentioned the courthouse. I dare say nobody will ever look at it. It's an enviable place. God Almighty Himself seems to watch over it. But you, Luka Lukich, as inspector of schools, ought to have an eye on the teachers. They are very learned gentlemen, no doubt, with a college education, but they have funny habits--inseparable from the profession, I know. One of them, for instance, the man with the fat face--I forget his name--is sure, the moment he takes his chair, to screw up his face like this. [Imitates him.] And then he has a trick of sticking his hand under his necktie and smoothing down his beard. It doesn't matter, of course, if he makes a face at the pupils; perhaps it's even necessary. I'm no judge of that. But you yourself will admit that if he does it to a visitor, it may turn out very badly. The Inspector, or anyone else, might take it as meant for himself, and then the deuce knows what might come of it.

LUKA. But what can I do? I have told him about it time and again. Only the other day when the marshal of the nobility came into the class-room, he made such a face at him as I had never in my life seen before. I dare say it was with the best intentions; But I get reprimanded for permitting radical ideas to be instilled in the minds of the young.

GOVERNOR. And then I must call your attention to the history teacher. He has a lot of learning in his head and a store of facts. That's evident. But he lectures with such ardor that he quite forgets himself. Once I listened to him. As long as he was talking about the Assyrians and Babylonians, it was not so bad. But when he reached Alexander of Macedon, I can't describe what came over him. Upon my word, I thought a fire had broken out. He jumped down from the platform, picked up a chair and dashed it to the floor. Alexander of Macedon was a hero, it is true. But that's no reason for breaking chairs. The state must bear the cost.

LUKA. Yes, he is a hot one. I have spoken to him about it several times. He only says: "As you please, but in the cause of learning I will even sacrifice my life."

GOVERNOR. Yes, it's a mysterious law of fate. Your clever man is either a drunkard, or he makes such grimaces that you feel like running away.

LUKA. Ah, Heaven save us from being in the educational department! One's afraid of everything. Everybody meddles and wants to show that he is as clever as you.

GOVERNOR. Oh, that's nothing. But this cursed incognito! All of a sudden he'll look in: "Ah, so you're here, my dear fellows! And who's the judge here?" says he. "Liapkin-Tiapkin." "Bring Liapkin-Tiapkin here.-- And who is the Superintendent of Charities?" "Zemlianika."--"Bring Zemlianika here!"-- That's what's bad.

SCENE II

Enter Ivan Kuzmich, the Postmaster.

POSTMASTER. Tell me, gentlemen, who's coming? What chinovnik?

GOVERNOR. What, haven't you heard?

POSTMASTER. Bobchinsky told me. He was at the postoffice just now.

GOVERNOR. Well, what do you think of it?

POSTMASTER. What do I think of it? Why, there'll be a war with the Turks.

AMMOS. Exactly. Just what I thought.

GOVERNOR [sarcastically]. Yes, you've both hit in the air precisely.

POSTMASTER. It's war with the Turks for sure, all fomented by the French.

GOVERNOR. Nonsense! War with the Turks indeed. It's we who are going to get it, not the Turks. You may count on that. Here's a letter to prove it.

POSTMASTER. In that case, then, we won't go to war with the Turks.

GOVERNOR. Well, how do you feel about it, Ivan Kuzmich?

POSTMASTER. How do I feel? How do YOU feel about it, Anton Antonovich?

GOVERNOR. I? Well, I'm not afraid, but I just feel a little--you know-- The merchants and townspeople bother me. I seem to be unpopular with them. But the Lord knows if I've taken from some I've done it without a trace of ill-feeling. I even suspect--[Takes him by the arm and walks aside with him.]--I even suspect that I may have been denounced. Or why would they send an Inspector to us? Look here, Ivan Kuzmich, don't you think you could--ahem!--just open a little every letter that passes through your office and read it-- for the common benefit of us all, you know--to see if it contains any kind of information against me, or is only ordinary correspondence. If it is all right, you can seal it up again, or simply deliver the letter opened.

POSTMASTER. Oh, I know. You needn't teach me that. I do it not so much as a precaution as out of curiosity. I just itch to know what's doing in the world. And it's very interesting reading, I tell you. Some letters are fascinating--parts of them written grand-- more edifying than the Moscow Gazette.

GOVERNOR. Tell me, then, have you read anything about any official from St. Petersburg?

POSTMASTER. No, nothing about a St. Petersburg official, but plenty about Kostroma and Saratov ones. A pity you don't read the letters. There are some very fine passages in them. For instance, not long ago a lieutenant writes to a friend describing a ball very wittily.-- Splendid! "Dear friend," he says, "I live in the regions of the Empyrean, lots of girls, bands playing, flags flying." He's put a lot of feeling into his description, a whole lot. I've kept the letter on purpose. Would you like to read it?

GOVERNOR. No, this is no time for such things. But please, Ivan Kuzmich, do me the favor, if ever you chance upon a complaint or denunciation, don't hesitate a moment, hold it back.

POSTMASTER. I will, with the greatest pleasure.

AMMOS. You had better be careful. You may get yourself into trouble.

POSTMASTER. Goodness me!

GOVERNOR. Never mind, never mind. Of course, it would be different if you published it broadcast. But it's a private affair, just between us.

AMMOS. Yes, it's a bad business--I really came here to make you a present of a puppy, sister to the dog you know about. I suppose you have heard that Cheptovich and Varkhovinsky have started a suit. So now I live in clover. I hunt hares first on the one's estate, then on the other's.

GOVERNOR. I don't care about your hares now, my good friend. That cursed incognito is on my brain. Any moment the door may open and in walk--

SCENE III

Enter Bobchinsky and Dobchinsky, out of breath.

BOBCHINSKY. What an extraordinary occurrence!

DOBCHINSKY. An unexpected piece of news!

ALL. What is it? What is it?

DOBCHINSKY. Something quite unforeseen. We were about to enter the inn--

BOBCHINSKY [interrupting]. Yes, Piotr Ivanovich and I were entering the inn--

DOBCHINSKY [interrupting]. Please, Piotr Ivanovich, let me tell.

BOBCHINSKY. No, please, let me--let me. You can't. You haven't got the style for it.

DOBCHINSKY. Oh, but you'll get mixed up and won't remember everything.

BOBCHINSKY. Yes, I will, upon my word, I will. PLEASE don't interrupt! Do let me tell the news--don't interrupt! Pray, oblige me, gentlemen, and tell Dobchinsky not to interrupt.

GOVERNOR. Speak, for Heaven's sake! What is it? My heart is in my mouth! Sit down, gentlemen, take seats. Piotr Ivanovich, here's a chair for you. [All seat themselves around Bobchinsky and Dobchinsky.] Well, now, what is it? What is it?

BOBCHINSKY. Permit me, permit me. I'll tell it all just as it happened. As soon as I had the pleasure of taking leave of you after you were good enough to be bothered with the letter which you had received, sir, I ran out--now, please don't keep interrupting, Dobchinsky. I know all about it, all, I tell you.-- So I ran out to see Korobkin. But not finding Korobkin at home, I went off to Rastakovsky, and not seeing him, I went to Ivan Kuzmich to tell him of the news you'd got. Going on from there I met Dobchinsky--

DOBCHINSKY [interjecting]. At the stall where they sell pies--

BOBCHINSKY. At the stall where they sell pies. Well, I met Dobchinsky and I said to him: "Have you heard the news that came to Anton Antonovich in a letter which is absolutely reliable?" But Piotr Ivanovich had already heard of it from your housekeeper, Avdotya, who, I don't know why, had been sent to Filipp Antonovich Pachechuyev--

DOBCHINSKY [interrupting]. To get a little keg for French brandy.

BOBCHINSKY. Yes, to get a little keg for French brandy. So then I went with Dobchinsky to Pachechuyev's.-- Will you stop, Piotr Ivanovich? Please don't interrupt.-- So off we went to Pachechuyev's, and on the way

Dobchinsky said: "Let's go to the inn," he said. "I haven't eaten a thing since morning. My stomach is growling." Yes, sir, his stomach was growling. "They've just got in a supply of fresh salmon at the inn," he said. "Let's take a bite." We had hardly entered the inn when we saw a young man--

DOBCHINSKY [Interrupting]. Of rather good appearance and dressed in ordinary citizen's clothes.

BOBCHINSKY. Yes, of rather good appearance and dressed in citizen's clothes--walking up and down the room. There was something out of the usual about his face, you know, something deep--and a manner about him--and here [raises his hand to his forehead and turns it around several times] full, full of everything. I had a sort of feeling, and I said to Dobchinsky, "Something's up. This is no ordinary matter." Yes, and Dobchinsky beckoned to the landlord, Vlas, the innkeeper, you know,--three weeks ago his wife presented him with a baby--a bouncer--he'll grow up just like his father and keep a tavern.-- Well, we beckoned to Vlas, and Dobchinsky asked him on the quiet, "Who," he asked, "is that young man?" "That young man," Vlas replied, "that young man"-- Oh, don't interrupt, Piotr Ivanovich, please don't interrupt. You can't tell the story. Upon my word, you can't. You lisp and one tooth in your mouth makes you whistle. I know what I'm saying. "That young man," he said, "is an official."-- Yes, sir.-- "On his way from St. Petersburg. And his name," he said, "is Ivan Aleksandrovich Khlestakov, and he's going," he said "to the government of Saratov," he said. "And he acts so queerly. It's the second week he's been here and he's never left the house; and he won't pay a penny, takes everything on account." When Vlas told me that, a light dawned on me from above, and I said to Piotr Ivanovich, "Hey!"--

DOBCHINSKY. No, Piotr Ivanovich, I said "HEY!"

BOBCHINSKY. Well first YOU said it, then I did. "Hey!" said both of us, "And why does he stick here if he's going to Saratov?"-- Yes, sir, that's he, the official.

GOVERNOR. Who? What official?

BOBCHINSKY. Why, the official who you were notified was coming, the Inspector.

GOVERNOR [terrified]. Great God! What's that you're saying. It can't be he.

DOBCHINSKY. It is, though. Why, he doesn't pay his bills and he doesn't leave. Who else can it be? And his postchaise is ordered for Saratov.

BOBCHINSKY. It's he, it's he, it's he--why, he's so alert, he scrutinized everything. He saw that Dobchinsky and I were eating salmon--chiefly on account of Dobchinsky's stomach--and he looked at our plates so hard that I was frightened to death.

GOVERNOR. The Lord have mercy on us sinners! In what room is he staying?

DOBCHINSKY. Room number 5 near the stairway.

BOBCHINSKY. In the same room that the officers quarreled in when they passed through here last year.

GOVERNOR. How long has he been here?

DOBCHINSKY. Two weeks. He came on St. Vasili's day.

GOVERNOR. Two weeks! [Aside.] Holy Fathers and saints preserve me! In those two weeks I have flogged the wife of a non-commissioned officer, the prisoners were not given their rations, the streets are dirty as a pothouse--a scandal, a disgrace! [Clutches his head with both hands.]

ARTEMY. What do you think, Anton Antonovich, hadn't we better go in state to the inn?

AMMOS. No, no. First send the chief magistrate, then the clergy, then the merchants. That's what it says in the book. The Acts of John the Freemason.

GOVERNOR. No, no, leave it to me. I have been in difficult situations before now. They have passed off all right, and I was even rewarded with thanks. Maybe the Lord will help us out this time, too. [Turns to Bobchinsky.] You say he's a young man?

BOBCHINSKY. Yes, about twenty-three or four at the most.

GOVERNOR. So much the better. It's easier to pump things out of a young man. It's tough if you've got a hardened old devil to deal with. But a young man is all on the surface. You, gentlemen, had better see to your end of things while I go unofficially, by myself, or with Dobchinsky here, as though for a walk, to see that the visitors that come to town are properly accommodated. Here, Svistunov. [To one of the Sergeants.]

SVISTUNOV. Sir.

GOVERNOR. Go instantly to the Police Captain--or, no, I'll want you. Tell somebody to send him here as quickly as possibly and then come back.

Svistunov hurries off.

ARTEMY. Let's go, let's go, Ammos Fiodorovich. We may really get into trouble.

AMMOS. What have you got to be afraid of? Put clean nightcaps on the patients and the thing's done.

ARTEMY. Nightcaps! Nonsense! The patients were ordered to have oatmeal soup. Instead of that there's such a smell of cabbage in all the corridors that you've got to hold your nose.

AMMOS. Well, my mind's at ease. Who's going to visit the court? Supposing he does look at the papers, he'll wish he had left them alone. I have been on the bench fifteen years, and when I take a look into a report, I despair. King Solomon in all his wisdom could not tell what is true and what is not true in it.

The Judge, the Superintendent of Charities, the School Inspector, and Postmaster go out and bump up against the Sergeant in the doorway as the latter returns.

SCENE IV

The Governor, Bobchinsky, Dobchinsky, and Sergeant Svistunov.

GOVERNOR. Well, is the cab ready?

SVISTUNOV. Yes, sir.

GOVERNOR. Go out on the street--or, no, stop--go and bring--why, where are the others? Why are you alone? Didn't I give orders for Prokhorov to be here? Where is Prokhorov?

SVISTUNOV. Prokhorov is in somebody's house and can't go on duty just now.

GOVERNOR. Why so?

SVISTUNOV. Well, they brought him back this morning dead drunk. They poured two buckets of water over him, but he hasn't sobered up yet.

GOVERNOR [clutching his head with both hands]. For Heaven's sake! Go out on duty quick--or, no, run up to my room, do you hear? And fetch my sword and my new hat. Now, Piotr Ivanovich, [to Dobchinsky] come.

BOBCHINSKY. And me--me, too. Let me come, too, Anton Antonovich.

GOVERNOR. No, no, Bobchinsky, it won't do. Besides there is not enough room in the cab.

BOBCHINSKY. Oh, that doesn't matter. I'll follow the cab on foot--on foot. I just want to peep through a crack--so--to see that manner of his-- how he acts.

GOVERNOR [turning to the Sergeant and taking his sword]. Be off and get the policemen together. Let them each take a--there, see how scratched my sword is. It's that dog of a merchant, Abdulin. He sees the Governor's sword is old and doesn't provide a new one. Oh, the sharpers! I'll bet they've got their petitions against me ready in their coat-tail pockets.--Let each take a street in his hand--I don't mean a street--a broom-- and sweep the street leading to the inn, and sweep it clean, and--do you hear? And see here, I know you, I know your tricks. You insinuate yourselves into the inn and walk off with silver spoons in your boots. Just you look out. I keep my ears pricked. What have you been up to with the merchant, Chorniayev, eh? He gave you two yards of cloth for your uniform and you stole the whole piece. Take care. You're only a Sergeant. Don't graft higher than your rank. Off with you.

SCENE V

Enter the Police Captain.

GOVERNOR. Hello, Stepan Ilyich, where the dickens have you been keeping yourself? What do you mean by acting that way?

CAPTAIN. Why, I was just outside the gate.

GOVERNOR. Well, listen, Stepan Ilyich. An official has come from St. Petersburg. What have you done about it?

CAPTAIN. What you told me to. I sent Sergeant Pugovichyn with policemen to clean the street.

GOVERNOR. Where is Derzhimorda?

CAPTAIN. He has gone off on the fire engine.

GOVERNOR. And Prokhorov is drunk?

CAPTAIN. Yes.

GOVERNOR. How could you allow him to get drunk?

CAPTAIN. God knows. Yesterday there was a fight outside the town. He went to restore order and was brought back drunk.

GOVERNOR. Well, then, this is what you are to do.-- Sergeant Pugovichyn--he is tall. So he is to stand on duty on the bridge for appearance' sake. Then the old fence near the bootmaker's must be pulled down at once and a post stuck up with a whisp of straw so as to look like grading. The more debris there is the more it will show the governor's activity.-- Good God, though, I forgot that about forty cart-loads of rubbish have been dumped against that fence. What a vile, filthy town this is! A monument, or even only a fence, is erected, and instantly they bring a lot of dirt together, from the devil knows where, and dump it there. [Heaves a sigh.] And if the functionary that has come here asks any of the officials whether they are satisfied, they are to say, "Perfectly satisfied, your Honor"; and if anybody is not satisfied, I'll give him something to be dissatisfied about afterwards.-- Ah, I'm a sinner, a terrible sinner. [Takes the hat-box, instead of his hat.] Heaven only grant that I may soon get this matter over and done with; then I'll donate a candle such as has never been offered before. I'll levy a hundred pounds of wax from every damned merchant. Oh my, oh my! Come, let's go, Piotr Ivanovich. [Tries to put the hat-box on his head instead of his hat.]

CAPTAIN. Anton Antonovich, that's the hat-box, not your hat.

GOVERNOR [throwing the box down]. If it's the hat-box, it's the hat-box, the deuce take it!-- And if he asks why the church at the hospital for which the money was appropriated five years ago has not been built, don't let them forget to say that the building was begun but was destroyed by fire. I sent in a report about it, you know. Some blamed fool might forget and let out that the building was never even begun. And tell Derzhimorda not to be so free with his fists. Guilty or innocent, he makes them all see stars in the cause of public order.-- Come on, come on, Dobchinsky. [Goes out and returns.] And don't let the soldiers appear on the streets with nothing on. That rotten garrison wear their coats directly over their undershirts.

All go out.

SCENE VI

Anna Andreyevna and Marya Antonovna rush in on the stage.

ANNA. Where are they? Where are they? Oh, my God! [opening the door.] Husband! Antosha! Anton! [hurriedly, to Marya.] It's all your fault. Dawdling! Dawdling!--"I want a pin--I want a scarf." [Runs to the window and calls.] Anton, where are you going? Where are you going? What! He has come? The Inspector? He has a moustache? What kind of a moustache?

GOVERNOR [from without]. Wait, dear. Later.

ANNA. Wait? I don't want to wait. The idea, wait! I only want one word. Is he a colonel or what? Eh? [Disgusted.] There, he's gone! You'll pay for it! It's all your fault--you, with your "Mamma, dear, wait a moment, I'll just pin my scarf. I'll come directly." Yes, directly! Now we have missed the news. It's all your confounded coquettishness. You heard the Postmaster was here and so you must prink and prim yourself in front of the mirror-- look on this side and that side and all around. You imagine he's smitten with you. But I can tell you he makes a face at you the moment you turn your back.

MARYA. It can't be helped, mamma. We'll know everything in a couple of hours anyway.

ANNA. In a couple of hours! Thank you! A nice answer. Why don't you say, in a month. We'll know still more in a month. [She leans out of the window.] Here, Avdotya! I say! Have you heard whether anybody has come, Avdotya?-- No, you goose, you didn't -- He waved his hands? Well, what of it? Let him wave his hands. But you should have asked him anyhow. You couldn't find out, of course, with your head full of nonsense and lovers. Eh, what? They left in a hurry? Well, you should have run after the carriage. Off with you, off with you at once, do you hear? Run and ask everybody where they are. Be sure and find out who the newcomer is and what he is like, do you hear? Peep through a crack and find everything out --what sort of eyes he has, whether they are black or blue, and be back here instantly, this minute, do you hear? Quick, quick, quick!

She keeps on calling and they both stand at the window until the curtain drops.

ACT II

A small room in the inn, bed, table, travelling bag, empty bottle, boots, clothes brush, etc.

SCENE I

OSIP [lying on his master's bed]. The devil take it! I'm so hungry. There's a racket in my belly, as if a whole regiment were blowing trumpets. We'll never reach home. I'd like to know what we are going to do. Two months already since we left St. Pete. He's gone through all his cash, the precious buck, so now he sticks here with his tail between his legs and takes it easy. We'd have had enough and more than enough to pay for the fare, but no he must exhibit himself in every town. [Imitates him.] "Osip, get me the best room to be had and order the best dinner they serve. I can't stand bad food. I must have the best." It would be all right for a somebody, but for a common copying clerk! Goes and gets acquainted with the other travellers, plays cards, and plays himself out of his last penny. Oh, I'm sick of this life. It's better in our village, really. There isn't so much going on, but then there is less to bother about. You get yourself a wife and lie on the stove all the time and eat pie. Of course, if you wanted to tell the truth, there's no denying it that there's nothing like living in St. Pete. All you want is money. And then you can live smart and classy--theeadres, dogs to dance for you, everything, and everybody talks so genteel, pretty near like in high society. If you go to the Schukin bazaar, the shopkeepers cry, "Gentlemen," at you.

You sit with the officials in the ferry boat. If you want company, you go into a shop. A sport there will tell you about life in the barracks and explain the meaning of every star in the sky, so that you see them all as if you held them in your hand. Then an old officer's wife will gossip, or a pretty chambermaid will dart a look at you--ta, ta, ta! [Smirks and wags his head.] And what deucedly civil manners they have, too. You never hear no impolite language. They always say "Mister" to you. If you are tired of walking, why you take a cab and sit in it like a lord. And if you don't feel like paying, then you don't. Every house has an open-work gate and you can slip through and the devil himself won't catch you. There's one bad thing, though; sometimes you get first class eats and sometimes you're so starved you nearly drop--like now. It's all his fault. What can you do with him? His dad sends him money to keep him going, but the devil a lot it does. He goes off on a spree, rides in cabs, gets me to buy a theeadre ticket for him every day, and in a week look at him--sends me to the old clo'es man to sell his new dress coat. Sometimes he gets rid of everything down to his last shirt and is left with nothing except his coat and overcoat. Upon my word, it's the truth. And such fine cloth, too. English, you know. One dress coat costs him a hundred and fifty rubles and he sells it to the old clo'es man for twenty. No use saying nothing about his pants. They go for a song. And why? Because he doesn't tend to his business. Instead of sticking to his job, he gads about on the Prospect and plays cards. Ah, if the old gentleman only knew it! He wouldn't care that you are an official. He'd lift up your little shirtie and would lay it on so that you'd go about rubbing yourself for a week. If you have a job, stick to it. Here's the innkeeper says he won't let you have anything to eat unless you pay your back bills. Well, and suppose we don't pay. [Sighing.] Oh, good God! If only I could get cabbage soup. I think I could eat up the whole world now. There's a knock at the door. I suppose it's him. [Rises from the bed hastily.]

SCENE II

Osip and Khlestakov.

KHLESTAKOV. Here! [Hands him his cap and cane.] What, been warming the bed again!

OSIP. Why should I have been warming the bed? Have I never seen a bed before?

KHLESTAKOV. You're lying. The bed's all tumbled up.

OSIP. What do I want a bed for? Don't I know what a bed is like? I have legs and can use them to stand on. I don't need your bed.

KHLESTAKOV [walking up and down the room]. Go see if there isn't some tobacco in the pouch.

OSIP. What tobacco? You emptied it out four days ago.

KHLESTAKOV [pacing the room and twisting his lips. Finally he says in a loud resolute voice]. Listen--a --Osip.

OSIP. Yes, sir?

KHLESTAKOV [In a voice just as loud, but not quite so resolute]. Go down there.

OSIP. Where?

KHLESTAKOV [in a voice not at all resolute, nor loud, but almost in entreaty]. Down to the restaurant--tell them--to send up dinner.

OSIP. No, I won't.

KHLESTAKOV. How dare you, you fool!

OSIP. It won't do any good, anyhow. The landlord said he won't let you have anything more to eat.

KHLESTAKOV. How dare he! What nonsense is this?

OSIP. He'll go to the Governor, too, he says. It's two weeks now since you've paid him, he says. You and your master are cheats, he says, and your master is a blackleg besides, he says. We know the breed. We've seen swindlers like him before.

KHLESTAKOV. And you're delighted, I suppose, to repeat all this to me, you donkey.

OSIP. "Every Tom, Dick and Harry comes and lives here," he says, "and runs up debts so that you can't even put him out. I'm not going to fool about it," he says, "I'm going straight to the Governor and have him arrested and put in jail."

KHLESTAKOV. That'll do now, you fool. Go down at once and tell him to have dinner sent up. The coarse brute! The idea!

OSIP. Hadn't I better call the landlord here?

KHLESTAKOV. What do I want the landlord for? Go and tell him yourself.

OSIP. But really, master--

KHLESTAKOV. Well, go, the deuce take you. Call the landlord.

Osip goes out.

SCENE III

KHLESTAKOV [alone]. I am so ravenously hungry. I took a little stroll thinking I could walk off my appetite. But, hang it, it clings. If I hadn't dissipated so in Penza I'd have had enough money to get home with. The infantry captain did me up all right. Wonderful the way the scoundrel cut the cards! It didn't take more than a quarter of an hour for him to clean me out of my last penny. And yet I would give anything to have another set-to with him. Only I never will have the chance.-- What a rotten town this is! You can't get anything on credit in the grocery shops here. It's deucedly mean, it is. [He whistles, first an air from Robert le Diable, then a popular song, then a blend of the two.] No one's coming.

SCENE IV

Khlestakov, Osip, and a Servant.

SERVANT. The landlord sent me up to ask what you want.

KHLESTAKOV. Ah, how do you do, brother! How are you? How are you?

SERVANT. All right, thank you.

KHLESTAKOV. And how are you getting on in the inn? Is business good?

SERVANT. Yes, business is all right, thank you.

KHLESTAKOV. Many guests?

SERVANT. Plenty.

KHLESTAKOV. See here, good friend. They haven't sent me dinner yet. Please hurry them up! See that I get it as soon as possible. I have some business to attend to immediately after dinner.

SERVANT. The landlord said he won't let you have anything any more. He was all for going to the Governor to-day and making a complaint against you.

KHLESTAKOV. What's there to complain about? Judge for yourself, friend. Why, I've got to eat. If I go on like this I'll turn into a skeleton. I'm hungry, I'm not joking.

SERVANT. Yes, sir, that's what he said. "I won't let him have no dinner," he said, "till he pays for what he has already had." That was his answer.

KHLESTAKOV. Try to persuade him.

SERVANT. But what shall I tell him?

KHLESTAKOV. Explain that it's a serious matter, I've got to eat. As for the money, of course-- He thinks that because a muzhik like him can go without food a whole day others can too. The idea!

SERVANT. Well, all right. I'll tell him.

The Servant and Osip go out.

SCENE V

Khlestakov alone.

KHLESTAKOV. A bad business if he refuses to let me have anything. I'm so hungry. I've never been so hungry in my life. Shall I try to raise something on my clothes? Shall I sell my trousers? No, I'd rather starve than come home without a St. Petersburg suit. It's a shame Joachim wouldn't let me have a carriage on hire. It would have been great to ride home in a carriage, drive up under the porte-cochere of one of the neighbors with lamps lighted and Osip behind in livery. Imagine the stir it would have created. "Who is it? What's that?" Then my footman walks in [draws himself up and imitates] and an- nounces: "Ivan Aleksandrovich Khlestakov of St. Petersburg. Will you receive him?" Those country lubbers don't even know what it means to "receive." If any lout of a country squire pays them a visit, he stalks straight into the drawing-room like a bear. Then you step up to one of their pretty girls and say: "Dee-lighted, madam." [Rubs his hands and bows.] Phew! [Spits.] I feel positively sick, I'm so hungry.

SCENE VI

Khlestakov, Osip, and later the Servant.

KHLESTAKOV. Well?

OSIP. They're bringing dinner.

KHLESTAKOV [claps his hands and wriggles in his chair]. Dinner, dinner, dinner!

SERVANT [with plates and napkin]. This is the last time the landlord will let you have dinner.

KHLESTAKOV. The landlord, the landlord! I spit on your landlord. What have you got there?

SERVANT. Soup and roast beef.

KHLESTAKOV. What! Only two courses?

SERVANT. That's all.

KHLESTAKOV. Nonsense! I won't take it. What does he mean by that? Ask him. It's not enough.

SERVANT. The landlord says it's too much.

KHLESTAKOV. Why is there no sauce?

SERVANT. There is none.

KHLESTAKOV. Why not? I saw them preparing a whole lot when I passed through the kitchen. And in the dining-room this morning two short little men were eating salmon and lots of other things.

SERVANT. Well, you see, there is some and there isn't.

KHLESTAKOV. Why "isn't"?

SERVANT. Because there isn't any.

KHLESTAKOV. What, no salmon, no fish, no cutlets?

SERVANT. Only for the better kind of folk.

KHLESTAKOV. You're a fool.

SERVANT. Yes, sir.

KHLESTAKOV. You measly suckling pig. Why can they eat and I not? Why the devil can't I eat, too? Am I not a guest the same as they?

SERVANT. No, not the same. That's plain.

KHLESTAKOV. How so?

SERVANT. That's easy. THEY pay, that's it.

KHLESTAKOV. I'm not going to argue with you, simpleton! [Ladles out the soup and begins to eat.] What, you call that soup? Simply hot water poured into a cup. No taste to it at all. It only stinks. I don't want it. Bring me some other soup.

SERVANT. All right. I'll take it away. The boss said if you didn't want it, you needn't take it.

KHLESTAKOV [putting his hand over the dishes]. Well, well, leave it alone, you fool. You may be used to treat other people this way, but I'm not that sort. I advise you not to try it on me. My God! What soup! [Goes on eating.] I don't think anybody in the world tasted such soup. Feathers floating on the top instead of butter. [Cuts the piece of chicken in the soup.] Oh, oh, oh! What a bird!--Give me the roast beef. There's a little soup left,

Osip. Take it. [Cuts the meat.] What sort of roast beef is this? This isn't roast beef.

SERVANT. What else is it?

KHLESTAKOV. The devil knows, but it isn't roast beef. It's roast iron, not roast beef. [Eats.] Scoundrels! Crooks! The stuff they give you to eat! It makes your jaws ache to chew one piece of it. [Picks his teeth with his fingers.] Villains! It's as tough as the bark of a tree. I can't pull it out no matter how hard I try. Such meat is enough to ruin one's teeth. Crooks! [Wipes his mouth with the napkin.] Is there nothing else?

SERVANT. No.

KHLESTAKOV. Scoundrels! Blackguards! They might have given some decent pastry, or something, the lazy good-for-nothings! Fleecing their guests! That's all they're good for.

[The Servant takes the dishes and carries them out accompanied by Osip.]

SCENE VII

Khlestakov alone.

KHLESTAKOV. It's just as if I had eaten nothing at all, upon my word. It has only whetted my appetite. If I only had some change to send to the market and buy some bread.

OSIP [entering]. The Governor has come, I don't know what for. He's inquiring about you.

KHLESTAKOV [in alarm]. There now! That inn- keeper has gone and made a complaint against me. Suppose he really claps me into jail? Well! If he does it in a gentlemanly way, I may-- No, no, I won't. The officers and the people are all out on the street and I set the fashion for them and the merchant's daughter and I flirted. No, I won't. And pray, who is he? How dare he, actually? What does he take me for? A tradesman? I'll tell him straight out, "How dare you? How--"

[The door knob turns and Khlestakov goes pale and shrinks back.]

SCENE VIII

Khlestakov, the Governor, and Dobchinsky.

The Governor advances a few steps and stops. They stare at each other a few moments wide-eyed and frightened.

GOVERNOR [recovering himself a little and saluting military fashion]. I have come to present my compliments, sir.

KHLESTAKOV [bows]. How do you do, sir?

GOVERNOR. Excuse my intruding.

KHLESTAKOV. Pray don't mention it.

GOVERNOR. It's my duty as chief magistrate of this town to see that visitors and persons of rank should suffer no inconveniences.

KHLESTAKOV [a little halting at first, but toward the end in a loud, firm voice]. Well--what was--to be-- done? It's not--my fault. I'm--really going to pay. They will send me money from home. [Bobchinsky peeps in at the door.] He's most to blame. He gives me beef as hard as a board and the soup--the devil knows what he put into it. I ought to have pitched it out of the window. He starves me the whole day. His tea is so peculiar--it smells of fish, not tea. So why should I-- The idea!

GOVERNOR [scared]. Excuse me! I assure you, it's not my fault. I always have good beef in the market here. The Kholmogory merchants bring it, and they are sober, well-behaved people. I'm sure I don't know where he gets his bad meat from. But if anything is wrong, may I suggest that you allow me to take you to another place?

KHLESTAKOV. No, I thank you. I don't care to leave. I know what the other place is--the jail. What right have you, I should like to know--how dare you?-- Why, I'm in the government service at St. Petersburg. [Puts on a bold front.] I--I--I--

GOVERNOR [aside]. My God, how angry he is. He has found out everything. Those damned merchants have told him everything.

KHLESTAKOV [with bravado]. I won't go even if you come here with your whole force. I'll go straight to the minister. [Bangs his fist on the table.] What do you mean? What do you mean?

GOVERNOR [drawing himself up stiffly and shaking all over]. Have pity on me. Don't ruin me. I have a wife and little children. Don't bring misfortune on a man.

KHLESTAKOV. No, I won't go. What's that got to do with me? Must I go to jail because you have a wife and little children? Great! [Bobchinsky looks in at the door and disappears in terror.] No, much obliged to you. I will not go.

GOVERNOR [trembling]. It was my inexperience. I swear to you, it was nothing but my inexperience and insufficient means. Judge for yourself. The salary I get is not enough for tea and sugar. And if I have taken bribes, they were mere trifles--something for the table, or a coat or two. As for the officer's widow to whom they say I gave a beating, she's in business now, and it's a slander, it's a slander that I beat her. Those scoundrels here invented the lie. They are ready to murder me. That's the kind of people they are.

KHLESTAKOV. Well. I've nothing to do with them. [Reflecting.] I don't see, though, why you should talk to me about your scoundrels or officer's widow. An officer's widow is quite a different matter.-- But don't you dare to beat me. You can't do it to me--no, sir, you can't. The idea! Look at him! I'll pay, I'll pay the money. Just now I'm out of cash. That's why I stay here--because I haven't a single kopek.

GOVERNOR [aside]. Oh, he's a shrewd one. So that's what he's aiming at? He's raised such a cloud of dust you can't tell what direction he's going. Who can guess what he wants? One doesn't know where to begin. But I will try. Come what may, I'll try--hit or miss. [Aloud.] H'm, if you really are in want of money, I'm ready to serve you. It is my duty to assist strangers in town.

KHLESTAKOV. Lend me some, lend me some. Then I'll settle up immediately with the landlord. I only want two hundred rubles. Even less would do.

GOVERNOR. There's just two hundred rubles. [Giving him the money.] Don't bother to count it.

KHLESTAKOV [taking it]. Very much obliged to you. I'll send it back to you as soon as I get home. I just suddenly found myself without-- H'm-- I see you are a gentleman. Now it's all different.

GOVERNOR [aside]. Well, thank the Lord, he's taken the money. Now I suppose things will move along smoothly. I slipped four hundred instead of two into his hand.

KHLESTAKOV. Ho, Osip! [Osip enters.] Tell the servant to come. [To the Governor and Dobchinsky.] Please be seated. [To Dobchinsky.] Please take a seat, I beg of you.

GOVERNOR. Don't trouble. We can stand.

KHLESTAKOV. But, please, please be seated. I now see perfectly how open-hearted and generous you are. I confess I thought you had come to put me in-- [To Dobchinsky.] Do take a chair.

The Governor and Dobchinsky sit down. Bobchinsky looks in at the door and listens.

GOVERNOR [aside]. I must be bolder. He wants us to pretend he is incognito. Very well, we will talk nonsense, too. We'll pretend we haven't the least idea who he is. [Aloud.] I was going about in the performance of my duty with Piotr Ivanovich Dobchinsky here-- he's a landed proprietor here--and we came to the inn to see whether the guests are properly accommodated-- because I'm not like other governors, who don't care about anything. No, apart from my duty, out of pure Christian philanthropy, I wish every mortal to be decently treated. And as if to reward me for my pains, chance has afforded me this pleasant acquaintance.

KHLESTAKOV. I, too, am delighted. Without your aid, I confess, I should have had to stay here a long time. I didn't know how in the world to pay my bill.

GOVERNOR [aside]. Oh, yes, fib on.-- Didn't know how to pay his bill! May I ask where your Honor is going?

KHLESTAKOV. I'm going to my own village in the Government of Saratov.

GOVERNOR [aside, with an ironical expression on his face]. The Government of Saratov! H'm, h'm! And doesn't even blush! One must be on the qui vive with this fellow. [Aloud.] You have undertaken a great task. They say travelling is disagreeable because of the delay in getting horses but, on the other hand, it is a diversion. You are travelling for your own amusement, I suppose?

KHLESTAKOV. No, my father wants me. He's angry because so far I haven't made headway in the St. Petersburg service. He thinks they stick the Vladimir in your buttonhole the minute you get there. I'd like him to knock about in the government offices for a while.

GOVERNOR [aside]. How he fabricates! Dragging in his old father, too. [Aloud.] And may I ask whether you are going there to stay for long?

KHLESTAKOV. I really don't know. You see, my father is stubborn and stupid--an old dotard as hard as a block of wood. I'll tell him straight out, "Do what you will, I can't live away from St. Petersburg." Really, why should I waste my life among peasants? Our times make different demands on us. My soul craves enlightenment.

GOVERNOR [aside]. He can spin yarns all right. Lie after lie and never trips. And such an ugly insignificant-looking creature, too. Why, it seems to me I could crush him with my finger nails. But wait, I'll make you talk. I'll make you tell me things. [Aloud.] You were quite right in your observation, that one can do nothing in a dreary out-of-the-way place. Take this town, for instance. You lie awake nights, you work hard for your country, you don't spare yourself, and the reward? You don't know when it's coming. [He looks round the room.] This room seems rather damp.

KHLESTAKOV. Yes, it's a dirty room. And the bugs! I've never experienced anything like them. They bite like dogs.

GOVERNOR. You don't say! An illustrious guest like you to be subjected to such annoyance at the hands of --whom? Of vile bugs which should never have been born. And I dare say, it's dark here, too.

KHLESTAKOV. Yes, very gloomy. The landlord has introduced the custom of not providing candles. Sometimes I want to do something--read a bit, or, if the fancy strikes me, write something.-- I can't. It's a dark room, yes, very dark.

GOVERNOR. I wonder if I might be bold enough to ask you--but, no, I'm unworthy.

KHLESTAKOV. What is it?

GOVERNOR. No, no, I'm unworthy. I'm unworthy.

KHLESTAKOV. But what is it?

GOVERNOR. If I might be bold enough--I have a fine room for you at home, light and cosy. But no, I feel it is too great an honor. Don't be offended. Upon my word, I made the offer out of the simplicity of my heart.

KHLESTAKOV. On the contrary, I accept your invitation with pleasure. I should feel much more comfortable in a private house than in this disreputable tavern.

GOVERNOR. I'm only too delighted. How glad my wife will be. It's my character, you know. I've always been hospitable from my very childhood, especially when my guest is a distinguished person. Don't think I say this out of flattery. No, I haven't that vice. I only speak from the fullness of my heart.

KHLESTAKOV. I'm greatly obliged to you. I myself hate double-faced people. I like your candor and kind-heartedness exceedingly. And I am free to say, I ask for nothing else than devotion and esteem--esteem and devotion.

SCENE IX

The above and the Servant, accompanied by Osip. Bobchinsky peeps in at the door.

SERVANT. Did your Honor wish anything?

KHLESTAKOV. Yes, let me have the bill.

SERVANT. I gave you the second one a little while ago.

KHLESTAKOV. Oh, I can't remember your stupid accounts. Tell me what the whole comes to.

SERVANT. You were pleased to order dinner the first day. The second day you only took salmon. And then you took everything on credit.

KHLESTAKOV. Fool! [Starts to count it all up now.] How much is it altogether?

GOVERNOR. Please don't trouble yourself. He can wait. [To the Servant.] Get out of here. The money will be sent to you.

KHLESTAKOV. Yes, that's so, of course. [He puts the money in his pocket.]

The Servant goes out. Bobchinsky peeps in at the door.

SCENE X

The Governor, Khlestakov and Dobchinsky.

GOVERNOR. Would you care to inspect a few institutions in our town now--the philanthropic institutions, for instance, and others?

KHLESTAKOV. But what is there to see?

GOVERNOR. Well, you'll see how they're run--the order in which we keep them.

KHLESTAKOV. Oh, with the greatest pleasure. I'm ready.

Bobchinsky puts his head in at the door.

GOVERNOR. And then, if you wish, we can go from there and inspect the district school and see our method of education.

KHLESTAKOV. Yes, yes, if you please.

GOVERNOR. Afterwards, if you should like to visit our town jails and prisons, you will see how our criminals are kept.

KHLESTAKOV. Yes, yes, but why go to prison? We had better go to see the philanthropic institutions.

GOVERNOR. As you please. Do you wish to ride in your own carriage, or with me in the cab?

KHLESTAKOV. I'd rather take the cab with you.

GOVERNOR [to Dobchinsky]. Now there'll be no room for you, Piotr Ivanovich.

DOBCHINSKY. It doesn't matter. I'll walk.

GOVERNOR [aside, to Dobchinsky]. Listen. Run as fast as you can and take two notes, one to Zemlianika at the hospital, the other to my wife. [To Khlestakov.] May I take the liberty of asking you to permit me to write a line to my wife to tell her to make ready to receive our honored guest?

KHLESTAKOV. Why go to so much trouble? However, there is the ink. I don't know whether there is any paper. Would the bill do?

GOVERNOR. Yes, that'll do. [Writes, talking to himself at the same time.] We'll see how things will go after lunch and several stout-bellied bottles. We have some Russian Madeira, not much to look at, but it will knock an elephant off its legs. If I only knew what he is and how much I have to be [on] my guard.

He finishes writing and gives the notes to Dobchinsky. As the latter walks across the stage, the door suddenly falls in, and Bobchinsky tumbles in with it to the floor. All exclaim in surprise. Bobchinsky rises.

KHLESTAKOV. Have you hurt yourself?

BOBCHINSKY. Oh, it's nothing--nothing at all-- only a little bruise on my nose. I'll run in to Dr. Hübner's. He has a sort of plaster. It'll soon pass away.

GOVERNOR [making an angry gesture at Bobchinsky. To Khlestakov]. Oh, it's nothing. Now, if you please, sir, we'll go. I'll tell your servant to carry your luggage over. [Calls Osip.] Here, my good fellow, take all your master's things to my house, the Governor's. Anyone will tell you where it is. By your leave, sir. [Makes way for Khlestakov and follows him; then turns and says reprovingly to Bobchinsky.] Couldn't you find some other place to fall in? Sprawling out here like a lobster!

Goes out. After him Bobchinsky. Curtain falls.

ACT III

SCENE: The same as in Act I.

SCENE I

Anna Andreyevna and Marya Antonovna standing at the window in the same positions as at the end of Act I.

ANNA. There now! We've been waiting a whole hour. All on account of your silly prinking. You were completely dressed, but no, you have to keep on dawdling.-- Provoking! Not a soul to be seen, as though on purpose, as though the whole world were dead.

MARYA. Now really, mamma, we shall know all about it in a minute or two. Avdotya must come back soon. [Looks out of the window and exclaims.] Oh, mamma, someone is coming--there down the street!

ANNA. Where? Just your imagination again!-- Why, yes, someone is coming. I wonder who it is. A short man in a frock coat. Who can it be? Eh? The suspense is awful! Who can it be, I wonder.

MARYA. Dobchinsky, mamma.

ANNA. Dobchinsky! Your imagination again! It's not Dobchinsky at all. [Waves her handkerchief.] Ho, you! Come here! Quick!

MARYA. It is Dobchinsky, mamma.

ANNA. Of course, you've got to contradict. I tell you, it's not Dobchinsky.

MARYA. Well, well, mamma? Isn't it Dobchinsky?

ANNA. Yes, it is, I see now. Why do you argue about it? [Calls through the window.] Hurry up, quick! You're so slow. Well, where are they? What? Speak from where you are. It's all the same. What? He is very strict? Eh? And how about my husband? [Moves away a little from the window, exasperated.] He is so stupid. He won't say a word until he is in the room.

SCENE II

Enter Dobchinsky.

ANNA. Now tell me, aren't you ashamed? You were the only one I relied on to act decently. They all ran away and you after them, and till now I haven't been able to find out a thing. Aren't you ashamed? I stood godmother to your Vanichka and Lizanko, and this is the way you treat me.

DOBCHINSKY. Godmother, upon my word, I ran so fast to pay my respects to you that I'm all out of breath. How do you do, Marya Antonovna?

MARYA. Good afternoon, Piotr Ivanovich.

ANNA. Well, tell me all about it. What is happening at the inn?

DOBCHINSKY. I have a note for you from Anton Antonovich.

ANNA. But who is he? A general?

DOBCHINSKY. No, not a general, but every bit as good as a general, I tell you. Such culture! Such dignified manners!

ANNA. Ah! So he is the same as the one my husband got a letter about.

DOBCHINSKY. Exactly. It was Piotr Ivanovich and I who first discovered him.

ANNA. Tell me, tell me all about it.

DOBCHINSKY. It's all right now, thank the Lord. At first he received Anton Antonovich rather roughly. He was angry and said the inn was not run properly, and he wouldn't come to the Governor's house and he didn't want to go to jail on account of him. But then when he found out that Anton Antonovich was not to blame and they got to talking more intimately, he changed right away, and, thank Heaven, everything went well. They've gone now to inspect the philanthropic institutions. I confess that Anton Antonovich had already begun to suspect that a secret denunciation had been lodged against him. I myself was trembling a little, too.

ANNA. What have you to be afraid of? You're not an official.

DOBCHINSKY. Well, you see, when a Grand Mogul speaks, you feel afraid.

ANNA. That's all rubbish. Tell me, what is he like personally? Is he young or old?

DOBCHINSKY. Young--a young man of about twenty-three. But he talks as if he were older. "If you will allow me," he says, "I will go there and there." [Waves his hands.] He does it all with such distinction. "I like," he says, "to read and write, but I am prevented because my room is rather dark."

ANNA. And what sort of a looking man is he, dark or fair?

DOBCHINSKY. Neither. I should say rather chestnut. And his eyes dart about like little animals. They make you nervous.

ANNA. Let me see what my husband writes. [Reads.] "I hasten to let you know, dear, that my position was extremely uncomfortable, but relying on the mercy of God, two pickles extra and a half portion of caviar, one ruble and twenty-five kopeks." [Stops.] I don't understand. What have pickles and caviar got to do with it?

DOBCHINSKY. Oh, Anton Antonovich hurriedly wrote on a piece of scrap paper. There's a kind of bill on it.

ANNA. Oh, yes, I see. [Goes on reading.] "But relying on the mercy of God, I believe all will turn out well in the end. Get a room ready quickly for the distinguished guest--the one with the gold wall paper. Don't bother to get any extras for dinner because we'll have something at the hospital with Artemy Filippovich. Order a little more wine, and tell Abdulin to send the best, or I'll wreck his whole cellar. I kiss your hand, my dearest, and remain yours, Anton Skvoznik-Dmukhanovsky." Oh my! I must hurry. Hello, who's there? Mishka?

DOBCHINSKY [Runs to the door and calls.] Mishka! Mishka! Mishka! [Mishka enters.]

ANNA. Listen! Run over to Abdulin--wait, I'll give you a note. [She sits down at the table and writes, talking all the while.] Give this to Sidor, the coachman, and tell him to take it to Abdulin and bring back the wine. And get to work at once and make the gold room ready for a guest. Do it nicely. Put a bed in it, a wash basin and pitcher and everything else.

DOBCHINSKY. Well, I'm going now, Anna Andreyevna, to see how he does the inspecting.

ANNA. Go on, I'm not keeping you.

SCENE III

Anna Andreyevna and Marya Antonovna.

ANNA. Now, Mashenka, we must attend to our toilet. He's a metropolitan swell and God forbid that he should make fun of us. You put on your blue dress with the little flounces. It's the most becoming.

MARYA. The idea, mamma! The blue dress! I can't bear it. Liapkin-Tiapkin's wife wears blue and so does Zemlianika's daughter. I'd rather wear my flowered dress.

ANNA. Your flowered dress! Of course, just to be contrary. You'll look lots better in blue because I'm going to wear my dun-colored dress. I love dun-color.

MARYA. Oh, mamma, it isn't a bit becoming to you.

ANNA. What, dun-color isn't becoming to me?

MARYA. No, not a bit. I'm positive it isn't. One's eyes must be quite dark to go with dun-color.

ANNA. That's nice! And aren't my eyes dark? They are as dark as can be. What nonsense you talk! How can they be anything but dark when I always draw the queen of clubs.

MARYA. Why, mamma, you are more like the queen of hearts.

ANNA. Nonsense! Perfect nonsense! I never was a queen of hearts. [She goes out hurriedly with Marya and speaks behind the scenes.] The ideas she gets into her head! Queen of hearts! Heavens! What do you think of that?

As they go out, a door opens through which Mishka sweeps dirt on to the stage. Osip enters from another door with a valise on his head.

SCENE IV

Mishka and Osip.

OSIP. Where is this to go?

MISHKA. In here, in here.

OSIP. Wait, let me fetch breath first. Lord! What a wretched life! On an empty stomach any load seems heavy.

MISHKA. Say, uncle, will the general be here soon?

OSIP. What general?

MISHKA. Your master.

OSIP. My master? What sort of a general is he?

MISHKA. Isn't he a general?

OSIP. Yes, he's a general, only the other way round.

MISHKA. Is that higher or lower than a real general?

OSIP. Higher.

MISHKA. Gee whiz! That's why they are raising such a racket about him here.

OSIP. Look here, young man, I see you're a smart fellow. Get me something to eat, won't you?

MISHKA. There isn't anything ready yet for the likes of you. You won't eat plain food. When your master takes his meal, they'll let you have the same as he gets.

OSIP. But have you got any plain stuff?

MISHKA. We have cabbage soup, porridge and pie.

OSIP. That's all right. We'll eat cabbage soup, porridge and pie, we'll eat everything. Come, help me with the valise. Is there another way to go out there?

MISHKA. Yes.

They both carry the valise into the next room.

SCENE V

The Sergeants open both folding doors. Khlestakov enters followed by the Governor, then the Superintendent of Charities, the Inspector of Schools, Dobchinsky and Bobchinsky with a plaster on his nose. The Governor points to a piece of paper lying on the floor, and the Sergeants rush to pick it up, pushing each other in their haste.

KHLESTAKOV. Excellent institutions. I like the way you show strangers everything in your town. In other towns they didn't show me a thing.

GOVERNOR. In other towns, I venture to observe, the authorities and officials look out for themselves more. Here, I may say, we have no other thought than to win the Government's esteem through good order, vigilance, and efficiency.

KHLESTAKOV. The lunch was excellent. I've positively overeaten. Do you set such a fine table every day?

GOVERNOR. In honor of so agreeable a guest we do.

KHLESTAKOV. I like to eat well. That's what a man lives for--to pluck the flowers of pleasure. What was that fish called?

ARTEMY [running up to him]. Labardan.

KHLESTAKOV. It was delicious. Where was it we had our lunch? In the hospital, wasn't it?

ARTEMY. Precisely, in the hospital.

KHLESTAKOV. Yes, yes, I remember. There were beds there. The patients must have gotten well. There don't seem to have been many of them.

ARTEMY. About ten are left. The rest recovered. The place is so well run, there is such perfect order. It may seem incredible to you, but ever since I've taken over the management, they all recover like flies. No sooner does a patient enter the hospital than he feels better. And we obtain this result not so much by medicaments as by honesty and orderliness.

GOVERNOR. In this connection may I venture to call your attention to what a brain-racking job the office of Governor is. There are so many matters he has to give his mind to just in connection with keeping the town clean and repairs and alterations. In a word, it is enough to upset the most competent person. But, thank God, all goes well. Another governor, of course, would look out for his own advantage. But believe me, even nights in bed I keep thinking: "Oh, God, how could I manage things in such a way that the government would observe my devotion to duty and be satisfied?" Whether the government will reward me or not, that of course, lies with them. At least I'll have a clear conscience. When the whole town is in order, the streets swept clean, the prisoners well kept, and few drunkards--what more do I want? Upon my word, I don't even crave honors. Honors, of course, are alluring; but as against the happiness which comes from doing one's duty, they are nothing but dross and vanity.

ARTEMY [aside]. Oh, the do-nothing, the scoundrel! How he holds forth! I wish the Lord had blessed me with such a gift!

KHLESTAKOV. That's so. I admit I sometimes like to philosophize, too. Sometimes it's prose, and sometimes it comes out poetry.

BOBCHINSKY [to Dobchinsky]. How true, how true it all is, Piotr Ivanovich. His remarks are great. It's evident that he is an educated man.

KHLESTAKOV. Would you tell me, please, if you have any amusements here, any circles where one could have a game of cards?

GOVERNOR [aside]. Ahem! I know what you are aiming at, my boy. [Aloud.] God forbid! Why, no one here has even heard of such a thing as card-playing circles. I myself have never touched a card. I don't know how to play. I can never look at cards with indifference, and if I happen to see a king of diamonds or some such thing, I am so disgusted I have to spit out. Once I made a house of cards for the children, and then I dreamt of those confounded things the whole night. Heavens! How can people waste their precious time over cards!

LUKA LUKICH [aside]. But he faroed me out of a hundred rubles yesterday, the rascal.

GOVERNOR. I'd rather employ my time for the benefit of the state.

KHLESTAKOV. Oh, well, that's rather going too far. It all depends upon the point of view. If, for instance, you pass when you have to treble stakes, then of course-- No, don't say that a game of cards isn't very tempting sometimes.

SCENE VI

The above, Anna Andreyevna and Marya Antonovna.

GOVERNOR. Permit me to introduce my family, my wife and daughter.

KHLESTAKOV [bowing]. I am happy, madam, to have the pleasure of meeting you.

ANNA. Our pleasure in meeting so distinguished a person is still greater.

KHLESTAKOV [showing off]. Excuse me, madam, on the contrary, my pleasure is the greater.

ANNA. Impossible. You condescend to say it to compliment me. Won't you please sit down?

KHLESTAKOV. Just to stand near you is bliss. But if you insist, I will sit down. I am so, so happy to be at your side at last.

ANNA. I beg your pardon, but I dare not take all the nice things you say to myself. I suppose you must have found travelling very unpleasant after living in the capital.

KHLESTAKOV. Extremely unpleasant. I am accustomed, comprenez-vous, to life in the fashionable world, and suddenly to find myself on the road, in dirty inns with dark rooms and rude people--I confess that if it were not for this chance which--[giving Anna a look and showing off] compensated me for everything--

ANNA. It must really have been extremely unpleasant for you.

KHLESTAKOV. At this moment, however, I find it exceedingly pleasant, madam.

ANNA. Oh, I cannot believe it. You do me much honor. I don't deserve it.

KHLESTAKOV. Why don't you deserve it? You do deserve it, madam.

ANNA. I live in a village.

KHLESTAKOV. Well, after all, a village too has something. It has its hills and brooks. Of course it's not to be compared with St. Petersburg. Ah, St. Petersburg! What a life, to be sure! Maybe you think I am only a copying clerk. No, I am on a friendly footing with the chief of our department. He slaps me on the back. "Come, brother," he says, "and have dinner with me." I just drop in the office for a couple of minutes to say this is to be done so, and that is to be done that way. There's a rat of a clerk there for copying letters who does nothing but scribble all the time--tr, tr-- They even wanted to make me a college assessor, but I think to myself, "What do I want it for?" And the doorkeeper flies after me on the stairs with the shoe brush. "Allow me to shine your boots for you, Ivan Aleksandrovich," he says. [To the Governor.] Why are you standing, gentleman? Please sit down.

{GOVERNOR. Our rank is such that we can very Together { well stand.
{ARTEMY. We don't mind standing. {LUKA. Please don't trouble.

KHLESTAKOV. Please sit down without the rank. [The Governor and the rest sit down.] I don't like ceremony. On the contrary, I always like to slip by unobserved. But it's impossible to conceal oneself, impossible. I no sooner show myself in a place than they say, "There goes Ivan Aleksandrovich!" Once I was even taken for the commander-in-chief. The soldiers rushed out of the guard-house and saluted. Afterwards an officer, an intimate acquaintance of mine, said to me: "Why, old chap, we completely mistook you for the commander-in-chief."

ANNA. Well, I declare!

KHLESTAKOV. I know pretty actresses. I've written a number of vaudevilles, you know. I frequently meet literary men. I am on an intimate footing with Pushkin. I often say to him: "Well, Pushkin, old boy, how goes it?" "So, so, partner," he'd reply, "as usual." He's a great original.

ANNA. So you write too? How thrilling it must be to be an author! You write for the papers also, I suppose?

KHLESTAKOV. Yes, for the papers, too. I am the author of a lot of works--The Marriage of Figaro, Robert le Diable, Norma. I don't even remember all the names. I did it just by chance. I hadn't meant to write, but a theatrical manager said, "Won't you please write something for me?" I thought to myself: "All right, why not?" So I did it all in one evening, surprised everybody. I am extraordinarily light of thought. All that has appeared under the name of Baron Brambeus was written by me, and the The Frigate of Hope and The Moscow Telegraph.

ANNA. What! So you are Brambeus?

KHLESTAKOV. Why, yes. And I revise and whip all their articles into shape. Smirdin gives me forty thousand for it.

ANNA. I suppose, then, that Yury Miroslavsky is yours too.

KHLESTAKOV. Yes, it's mine.

ANNA. I guessed at once.

MARYA. But, mamma, it says that it's by Zagoskin.

ANNA. There! I knew you'd be contradicting even here.

KHLESTAKOV. Oh, yes, it's so. That was by Zagoskin. But there is another Yury Miroslavsky which was written by me.

ANNA. That's right. I read yours. It's charming.

KHLESTAKOV. I admit I live by literature. I have the first house in St. Petersburg. It is well known as the house of Ivan Aleksandrovich. [Addressing the company in general.] If any of you should come to St. Petersburg, do please call to see me. I give balls, too, you know.

ANNA. I can guess the taste and magnificence of those balls.

KHLESTAKOV. Immense! For instance, watermelon will be served costing seven hundred rubles. The soup comes in the tureen straight from Paris by steamer. When the lid is raised, the aroma of the steam is like nothing else in the world. And we have formed a circle for playing whist-- the Minister of Foreign Affairs, the French, the English and the German Ambassadors and myself. We play so hard we kill ourselves over the cards. There's nothing like it. After it's over I'm so tired I run home up the stairs to the fourth floor and tell the cook, "Here, Marushka, take my coat"-- What am I talking about?--I forgot that I live on the first floor. One flight up costs me-- My foyer before I rise in the morning is an interesting spectacle indeed--counts and princes jostling each other and humming like bees. All you hear is buzz, buzz, buzz. Sometimes the Minister-- [The Governor and the rest rise in awe from their chairs.] Even my mail comes addressed "Your Excellency." And once I even had charge of a department. A strange thing happened. The head of the department went off, disappeared, no one knew where. Of course there was a lot of talk about how the place would be filled, who would fill it, and all that sort of thing. There were ever so many generals hungry for the position, and they tried, but they couldn't cope with it. It's too hard. Just on the surface it looks easy enough; but when you come to examine it closely, it's the devil of a job. When they saw they couldn't manage, they came to me. In an instant the streets were packed full with couriers, nothing but couriers and couriers-- thirty-five thousand of them, imagine! Pray, picture the situation to yourself! "Ivan Aleksandrovich, do come and take the directorship of the department." I admit I was a little embarrassed. I came out in my dressing-gown. I wanted to decline, but I thought it might reach the Czar's ears, and, besides, my official record-- "Very well, gentlemen," I said, "I'll accept the position, I'll accept. So be it. But mind," I said, "na-na-na, LOOK SHARP is the word with me, LOOK SHARP!" And so it was. When I went through the offices of my department, it was a regular earthquake, Everyone trembled and shook like a leaf. [The Governor and the rest tremble with fright. Khlestakov works himself up more and more as he speaks.] Oh, I don't like to joke. I got all of them thoroughly scared, I tell you. Even the Imperial Council is afraid of me. And really, that's the sort I am. I don't spare anybody. I tell them all, "I know myself, I know myself." I am everywhere, everywhere. I go to Court daily. Tomorrow they are going to make me a field-marsh--

He slips and almost falls, but is respectfully held up by the officials.

GOVERNOR [walks up to him trembling from top to toe and speaking with a great effort]. Your Ex-ex-ex-

KHLESTAKOV [curtly]. What is it?

GOVERNOR. Your Ex-ex-ex-

KHLESTAKOV [as before]. I can't make out a thing, it's all nonsense.

GOVERNOR. Your Ex-ex--Your 'lency-- Your Excellency, wouldn't you like to rest a bit? Here's a room and everything you may need.

KHLESTAKOV. Nonsense--rest! However, I'm ready for a rest. Your lunch was fine, gentlemen. I am satisfied, I am satisfied. [Declaiming.] Labardan! Labardan!

He goes into the next room followed by the Governor.

SCENE VII

The same without Khlestakov and the Governor.

BOBCHINSKY [to Dobchinsky]. There's a man for you, Piotr Ivanovich. That's what I call a man. I've never in my life been in the presence of so important a personage. I almost died of fright. What do you think is his rank, Piotr Ivanovich?

DOBCHINSKY. I think he's almost a general.

BOBCHINSKY. And I think a general isn't worth the sole of his boots. But if he is a general, then he must be the generalissimo himself. Did you hear how he bullies the Imperial Council? Come, let's hurry off to Ammos Fiodorovich and Korobkin and tell them about it. Good-by, Anna Andreyevna.

DOBCHINSKY. Good afternoon, godmother.

Both go out.

ARTEMY. It makes your heart sink and you don't know why. We haven't even our uniforms on. Suppose after he wakes up from his nap he goes and sends a report about us to St. Petersburg. [He goes out sunk in thought, with the School Inspector, both saying.] Good-by, madam.

SCENE VIII

Anna Andreyevna and Marya Antonovna.

ANNA. Oh, how charming he is!

MARYA. A perfect dear!

ANNA. Such refined manners. You can recognize the big city article at once. How he carries himself, and all that sort of thing! Exquisite! I'm just crazy for young men like him. I am in ecstasies--beside myself. He liked me very much though. I noticed he kept looking at me all the time.

MARYA. Oh, mamma, he looked at me.

ANNA. No more nonsense please. It's out of place now.

MARYA. But really, mamma, he did look at me.

ANNA. There you go! For God's sake, don't argue. You mustn't. That's enough. What would he be looking at you for? Please tell me, why would he be looking at you?

MARYA. It's true, mamma. He kept looking at me. He looked at me when he began to speak about literature and he looked at me afterwards, when he told about how he played whist with the ambassadors.

ANNA. Well, maybe he looked at you once or twice and might have said to himself, "Oh, well, I'll give her a look."

SCENE IX

The same and the Governor.

GOVERNOR. Sh-sh!

ANNA. What is it?

GOVERNOR. I wish I hadn't given him so much to drink. Suppose even half of what he said is true? [Sunk in thought.] How can it not be true? A man in his cups is always on the surface. What's in his heart is on his tongue. Of course he fibbed a little. No talking is possible without some lying. He plays cards with the ministers and he visits the Court. Upon my word the more you think the less you know what's going on in your head. I'm as dizzy as if I were standing in a belfry, or if I were going to be hanged, the devil take it!

ANNA. And I didn't feel the least bit afraid. I simply saw a high-toned, cultured man of the world, and his rank and titles didn't make me feel a bit queer.

GOVERNOR. Oh, well, you women. To say women and enough's said. Everything is froth and bubble to you. All of a sudden you blab out words that don't make the least sense. The worst you'd get would be a flogging; but it means ruination to the husband.-- Say, my dear, you are as familiar with him as if he were another Bobchinsky.

ANNA. Leave that to us. Don't bother about that. [Glancing at Marya.] We know a thing or two in that line.

GOVERNOR [to himself]. Oh, what's the good of talking to you! Confound it all! I can't get over my fright yet. [Opens the door and calls.] Mishka, tell the sergeants, Svistunov and Derzhimorda, to come here. They are near the gate. [After a pause of silence.] The world has turned into a queer place. If at least the people were visible so you could see them; but they are such a skinny, thin race. How in the world could you tell what he is? After all you can tell a military man; but when he wears a frock-coat, it's like a fly with clipped wings. He kept it up a long time in the inn, got off a lot of allegories and ambiguities so that you couldn't make out head or tail. Now he's shown himself up at last.-- Spouted even more than necessary. It's evident that he's a young man.

SCENE X

The same and Osip. All rush to meet Osip, beckoning to him.

ANNA. Come here, my good man.

GOVERNOR. Hush! Tell me, tell me, is he asleep?

OSIP. No, not yet. He's stretching himself a little.

ANNA. What's your name?

OSIP. Osip, madam.

GOVERNOR [to his wife and daughter]. That'll do, that'll do. [To Osip.] Well, friend, did they give you a good meal?

OSIP. Yes, sir, very good. Thank you kindly.

ANNA. Your master has lots of counts and princes visiting him, hasn't he?

OSIP [aside]. What shall I say? Seeing as they've given me such good feed now, I s'pose they'll do even better later. [Aloud.] Yes, counts do visit him.

MARYA. Osip, darling, isn't your master just grand?

ANNA. Osip, please tell me, how is he--

GOVERNOR. Do stop now. You just interfere with your silly talk. Well, friend, how--

ANNA. What is your master's rank?

OSIP. The usual rank.

GOVERNOR. For God's sake, your stupid questions keep a person from getting down to business. Tell me, friend, what sort of a man is your master? Is he strict? Does he rag and bully a fellow--you know what I mean--does he or doesn't he?

OSIP. Yes, he likes things to be just so. He insists on things being just so.

GOVERNOR. I like your face. You must be a fine man, friend. What--?

ANNA. Listen, Osip, does your master wear uniform in St. Petersburg?

GOVERNOR. Enough of your tattle now, really. This is a serious matter, a matter of life and death. (To Osip.) Yes, friend, I like you very much. It's rather chilly now and when a man's travelling an extra glass of tea or so is rather welcome. So here's a couple of rubles for some tea.

OSIP [taking the money.] Thank you, much obliged to you, sir. God grant you health and long life. You've helped a poor man.

GOVERNOR. That's all right. I'm glad to do it. Now, friend--

ANNA. Listen, Osip, what kind of eyes does your master like most?

MARYA. Osip, darling, what a dear nose your master has!

GOVERNOR. Stop now, let me speak. [To Osip.] Tell me, what does your master care for most? I mean, when he travels what does he like?

OSIP. As for sights, he likes whatever happens to come along. But what he likes most of all is to be received well and entertained well.

GOVERNOR. Entertained well?

OSIP. Yes, for instance, I'm nothing but a serf and yet he sees to it that I should be treated well, too. S'help me God! Say we'd stop at some place and he'd ask, "Well, Osip, have they treated you well?" "No, badly, your Excellency." "Ah," he'd say, "Osip, he's not a good host. Remind me when we get home." "Oh, well," thinks I to myself [with a wave of his hand]. "I am a simple person. God be with them."

GOVERNOR. Very good. You talk sense. I've given you something for tea. Here's something for buns, too.

OSIP. You are too kind, your Excellency. [Puts the money in his pocket.] I'll sure drink your health, sir.

ANNA. Come to me, Osip, and I'll give you some, too.

MARYA. Osip, darling, kiss your master for me.

Khlestakov is heard to give a short cough in the next room.

GOVERNOR. Hush! [Rises on tip-toe. The rest of the conversation in the scene is carried on in an undertone.] Don't make a noise, for heaven's sake! Go, it's enough.

ANNA. Come, Mashenka, I'll tell you something I noticed about our guest that I can't tell you unless we are alone together. [They go out.]

GOVERNOR. Let them talk away. If you went and listened to them, you'd want to stop up your ears. [To Osip.] Well, friend--

SCENE XI

The same, Derzhimorda and Svistunov.

GOVERNOR. Sh--sh! Bandy-legged bears-- thumping their boots on the floor! Bump, bump as if a thousand pounds were being unloaded from a wagon. Where in the devil have you been knocking about?

DERZHIMORDA. I had your order--

GOVERNOR. Hush! [Puts his hand over Derzhimorda's mouth.] Like a bull bellowing. [Mocking him.] "I had your order--" Makes a noise like an empty barrel. [To Osip.] Go, friend, and get everything ready for your master. And you two, you stand on the steps and don't you dare budge from the spot. And don't let any strangers enter the house, especially the merchants. If you let a single one in, I'll-- The instant you see anybody with a petition, or even without a petition and he looks as if he wanted to present a petition against me, take him by the scruff of the neck, give him a good kick, [shows with his foot] and throw him out. Do you hear? Hush-- hush!

He goes out on tiptoe, preceded by the Sergeants.

CURTAIN

ACT IV

SCENE: Same as in Act III.

SCENE I

Enter cautiously, almost on tiptoe, Ammos Fiodorovich, Artemy Filippovich, the Postmaster, Luka Lukich, Dobchinsky and Bobchinsky in full dress-uniform.

AMMOS. For God's sake, gentlemen, quick, form your line, and let's have more order. Why, man alive, he goes to Court and rages at the Imperial Council. Draw up in military line, strictly in military line. You, Piotr Ivanovich, take your place there, and you, Piotr Ivanovich, stand here. [Both the Piotr Ivanoviches run on tiptoe to the places indicated.]

ARTEMY. Do as you please, Ammos Fiodorovich, I think we ought to try.

AMMOS. Try what?

ARTEMY. It's clear what.

AMMOS. Grease?

ARTEMY. Exactly, grease.

AMMOS. It's risky, the deuce take it. He'll fly into a rage at us. He's a government official, you know. Perhaps it should be given to him in the form of a gift from the nobility for some sort of memorial?

POSTMASTER. Or, perhaps, tell him some money has been sent here by post and we don't know for whom?

ARTEMY. You had better look out that he doesn't send you by post a good long ways off. Look here, things of such a nature are not done this way in a well-ordered state. What's the use of a whole regiment here? We must present ourselves to him one at a time, and do--what ought to be done, you know--so that eyes do not see and ears do not hear. That's the way things are done in a well-ordered society. You begin it, Ammos Fiodorovich, you be the first.

AMMOS. You had better go first. The distinguished guest has eaten in your institution.

ARTEMY. Then Luka Lukich, as the enlightener of youth, should go first.

LUKA. I can't, I can't, gentlemen. I confess I am so educated that the moment an official a single degree higher than myself speaks to me, my heart stands still and I get as tongue-tied as though my tongue were caught in the mud. No, gentlemen, excuse me. Please let me off.

ARTEMY. It's you who have got to do it, Ammos Fiodorovich. There's no one else. Why, every word you utter seems to be issuing from Cicero's mouth.

AMMOS. What are you talking about! Cicero! The idea! Just because a man sometimes waxes enthusiastic over house dogs or hunting hounds.

ALL [pressing him]. No, not over dogs, but the Tower of Babel, too. Don't forsake us, Ammos Fiodorovich, help us. Be our Saviour!

AMMOS. Let go of me, gentlemen.

Footsteps and coughing are heard in Khlestakov's room. All hurry to the door, crowding and jostling in their struggle to get out. Some are uncomfortably squeezed, and half-suppressed cries are heard.

BOBCHINSKY'S VOICE. Oh, Piotr Ivanovich, you stepped on my foot.

ARTEMY. Look out, gentlemen, look out. Give me a chance to atone for my sins. You are squeezing me to death.

Exclamations of "Oh! Oh!" Finally they all push through the door, and the stage is left empty.

SCENE II

Enter Khlestakov, looking sleepy.

KHLESTAKOV [alone]. I seem to have had a fine snooze. Where did they get those mattresses and feather beds from? I even perspired. After the meal yesterday they must have slipped something into me that knocked me out. I still feel a pounding in my head. I see I can have a good time here. I like hospitality, and I must say I like it all the more if people entertain me out of a pure heart and not from interested motives. The Governor's daughter is not a bad one at all, and the mother is also a woman you can still-- I don't know, but I do like this sort of life.

SCENE III

Khlestakov and the Judge.

JUDGE [comes in and stops. Talking to himself]. Oh, God, bring me safely out of this! How my knees are knocking together! [Drawing himself up and holding the sword in his hand. Aloud.] I have the honor to present myself--Judge of the District Court here, College Assessor Liapkin-Tiapkin.

KHLESTAKOV. Please be seated. So you are the Judge here?

JUDGE. I was elected by the nobility in 1816 and I have served ever since.

KHLESTAKOV. Does it pay to be a judge?

JUDGE. After serving three terms I was decorated with the Vladimir of the third class with the approval of the government. [Aside.] I have the money in my hand and my hand is on fire.

KHLESTAKOV. I like the Vladimir. Anna of the third class is not so nice.

JUDGE [slightly extending his balled fist. Aside]. Good God! I don't know where I'm sitting. I feel as though I were on burning coals.

KHLESTAKOV. What have you got in your hand there?

AMMOS [getting all mixed up and dropping the bills on the floor]. Nothing.

KHLESTAKOV. How so, nothing? I see money has dropped out of it.

AMMOS [shaking all over]. Oh no, oh no, not at all! [Aside.] Oh, Lord! Now I'm under arrest and they've brought a wagon to take me.

KHLESTAKOV. Yes, it IS money. [Picking it up.]

AMMOS [aside]. It's all over with me. I'm lost! I'm lost!

KHLESTAKOV. I tell you what--lend it to me.

AMMOS [eagerly]. Why, of course, of course--with the greatest pleasure. [Aside.] Bolder! Bolder! Holy Virgin, stand by me!

KHLESTAKOV. I've run out of cash on the road, what with one thing and another, you know. I'll let you have it back as soon as I get to the village.

AMMOS. Please don't mention it! It is a great honor to have you take it. I'll try to deserve it--by putting forth the best of my feeble powers, by my zeal and ardor for the government. [Rises from the chair and draws himself up straight with his hands hanging at his sides.] I will not venture to disturb you longer with my presence. You don't care to give any orders?

KHLESTAKOV. What orders?

JUDGE. I mean, would you like to give orders for the district court here?

KHLESTAKOV. What for? I have nothing to do with the court now. No, nothing. Thank you very much.

AMMOS [bowing and leaving. Aside.]. Now the town is ours.

KHLESTAKOV. The Judge is a fine fellow.

SCENE IV

Khlestakov and the Postmaster.

POSTMASTER [in uniform, sword in hand. Drawing himself up]. I have the honor to present myself-- Postmaster, Court Councilor Shpekin.

KHLESTAKOV. I'm glad to meet you. I like pleasant company very much. Take a seat. Do you live here all the time?

POSTMASTER. Yes, sir. Quite so.

KHLESTAKOV. I like this little town. Of course, there aren't many people. It's not very lively. But what of it? It isn't the capital. Isn't that so-- it isn't the capital?

POSTMASTER. Quite so, quite so.

KHLESTAKOV. It's only in the capital that you find bon-ton and not a lot of provincial lubbers. What is your opinion? Isn't that so?

POSTMASTER. Quite so. [Aside.] He isn't a bit proud. He inquires about everything.

KHLESTAKOV. And yet you'll admit that one can live happily in a little town.

POSTMASTER. Quite so.

KHLESTAKOV. In my opinion what you want is this --you want people to respect you and to love you sincerely. Isn't that so?

POSTMASTER. Exactly.

KHLESTAKOV. I'm glad you agree with me. Of course, they call me queer. But that's the kind of character I am. [Looking him in the face and talking to himself.] I think I'll ask this postmaster for a loan. [Aloud.] A strange accident happened to me and I ran out of cash on the road. Can you lend me three hundred rubles?

POSTMASTER. Of course. I shall esteem it a piece of great good fortune. I am ready to serve you with all my heart.

KHLESTAKOV. Thank you very much. I must say, I hate like the devil to deny myself on the road. And why should I? Isn't that so?

POSTMASTER. Quite so. [Rises, draws himself up, with his sword in his hand.] I'll not venture to disturb you any more. Would you care to make any remarks about the post office administration?

KHLESTAKOV. No, nothing.

The Postmaster bows and goes out.

KHLESTAKOV [lighting a cigar]. It seems to me the Postmaster is a fine fellow, too. He's certainly obliging. I like people like that.

SCENE V

Khlestakov and Luka Lukich, who is practically pushed in on the stage. A voice behind him is heard saying nearly aloud, "Don't be chickenhearted."

LUKA [drawing himself up, trembling, with his hand on his sword]. I have the honor to present myself-- School Inspector, Titular Councilor Khlopov.

KHLESTAKOV. I'm glad to see you. Take a seat, take a seat. Will you have a cigar? [Offers him a cigar.]

LUKA [to himself, hesitating]. There now! That's something I hadn't anticipated. To take or not to take?

KHLESTAKOV. Take it, take it. It's a pretty good cigar. Of course not what you get in St. Petersburg. There I used to smoke twenty-five cent cigars. You feel like kissing yourself after having smoked one of them. Here, light it. [Hands him a candle.]

Luka Lukich tries to light the cigar shaking all over.

KHLESTAKOV. Not that end, the other.

LUKA [drops the cigar from fright, spits and shakes his hands. Aside]. Confound it! My damned timidity has ruined me!

KHLESTAKOV. I see you are not a lover of cigars. I confess smoking is my weakness--smoking and the fair sex. Not for the life of me can I remain indifferent to the fair sex. How about you? Which do you like more, brunettes or blondes?

Luka Lukich remains silent, at a complete loss what to say.

KHLESTAKOV. Tell me frankly, brunettes or blondes?

LUKA. I don't dare to know.

KHLESTAKOV. No, no, don't evade. I'm bound to know your taste.

LUKA. I venture to report to you-- [Aside.] I don't know what I'm saying.

KHLESTAKOV. Ah, you don't want to say. I suppose some little brunette or other has cast a spell over you. Confess, she has, hasn't she?

Luka Lukich remains silent.

KHLESTAKOV. Ah, you're blushing. You see. Why don't you speak?

LUKA. I'm scared, your Hon--High--Ex-- [Aside.] Done for! My confounded tongue has undone me!

KHLESTAKOV. You're scared? There IS something awe-inspiring in my eyes, isn't there? At least I know not a single woman can resist them. Isn't that so?

LUKA. Exactly.

KHLESTAKOV. A strange thing happened to me on the road. I ran entirely out of cash. Can you lend me three hundred rubles?

LUKA [clutching his pockets. Aside]. A fine business if I haven't got the money! I have! I have! [Takes out the bills and gives them to him, trembling.]

KHLESTAKOV. Thank you very much.

LUKA [drawing himself up, with his hand on his sword]. I will not venture to disturb you with my presence any longer.

KHLESTAKOV. Good-by.

LUKA [dashes out almost at a run, saying aside.] Well, thank the Lord! Maybe he won't inspect the schools.

SCENE VI

Khlestakov and Artemy Filippovich.

ARTEMY [enters and draws himself up, his hand on his sword]. I have the honor to present myself-- Superintendent of Charities, Court Councilor Zemlianika.

KHLESTAKOV. Howdeedo? Please sit down.

ARTEMY. I had the honor of receiving you and personally conducting you through the philanthropic institutions committed to my care.

KHLESTAKOV. Oh, yes, I remember. You treated me to a dandy lunch.

ARTEMY. I am glad to do all I can in behalf of my country.

KHLESTAKOV. I admit, my weakness is a good cuisine.-- Tell me, please, won't you--it seems to me you were a little shorter yesterday, weren't you?

ARTEMY. Quite possible. [After a pause.] I may say I spare myself no pains and perform the duties of my office with the utmost zeal. [Draws his chair closer and speaks in a lowered tone.] There's the postmaster, for example, he does absolutely nothing. Everything is in a fearful state of neglect. The mail is held up. Investigate for yourself, if you please, and you will see. The Judge, too, the man who was here just now, does nothing but hunt hares, and he keeps his dogs in the court rooms, and his conduct, if I must confess--and for the benefit of the fatherland, I must confess, though he is my relative and friend--his conduct is in the highest degree reprehensible. There is a squire here by the name of Dobchinsky, whom you were pleased to see. Well, the moment Dobchinsky leaves the house, the Judge is there with Dobchinsky's wife. I can swear to it. You just take a look at the children. Not one of them resembles Dobchinsky. All of them, even the little girl, are the very image of the Judge.

KHLESTAKOV. You don't say so. I never imagined it.

ARTEMY. Then take the School Inspector here. I don't know how the government could have entrusted him with such an office. He's worse than a Jacobin freethinker, and he instils such pernicious ideas into the minds of the young that I can hardly describe it. Hadn't I better put it all down on paper, if you so order?

KHLESTAKOV. Very well, why not? I should like it very much. I like to kill the weary hours reading something amusing, you know. What is your name? I keep forgetting.

ARTEMY. Zemlianika.

KHLESTAKOV. Oh, yes, Zemlianika. Tell me, Mr. Zemlianika, have you any children?

ARTEMY. Of course. Five. Two are already grown up.

KHLESTAKOV. You don't say! Grown up! And how are they--how are they--a--a?

ARTEMY. You mean that you deign to ask what their names are?

KHLESTAKOV. Yes, yes, what are their names?

ARTEMY. Nikolay, Ivan, Yelizaveta, Marya and Perepetuya.

KHLESTAKOV. Good.

ARTEMY. I don't venture to disturb you any longer with my presence and rob you of your time dedicated to the performance of your sacred duties--- [Bows and makes to go.]

KHLESTAKOV [escorting him]. Not at all. What you told me is all very funny. Call again, please. I like that sort of thing very much. [Turns back and reopens the door, calling.] I say, there! What is your---- I keep forgetting. What is your first name and your patronymic?

ARTEMY. Artemy Filippovich.

KHLESTAKOV. Do me a favor, Artemy Filippovich. A curious accident happened to me on the road. I've run entirely out of cash. Have you four hundred rubles to lend me?

ARTEMY. I have.

KHLESTAKOV. That comes in pat. Thank you very much.

SCENE VII

Khlestakov, Bobchinsky, and Dobchinsky.

BOBCHINSKY. I have the honor to present myself --a resident of this town, Piotr, son of Ivan Bobchinsky.

DOBCHINSKY. I am Piotr, son of Ivan Dobchinsky, a squire.

KHLESTAKOV. Oh, yes, I've met you before. I believe you fell? How's your nose?

BOBCHINSKY. It's all right. Please don't trouble. It's dried up, dried up completely.

KHLESTAKOV. That's nice. I'm glad it's dried up. [Suddenly and abruptly.] Have you any money?

DOBCHINSKY. Money? How's that--money?

KHLESTAKOV. A thousand rubles to lend me.

BOBCHINSKY. Not so much as that, honest to God I haven't. Have you, Piotr Ivanovich?

DOBCHINSKY. I haven't got it with me, because my money--I beg to inform you--is deposited in the State Savings Bank.

KHLESTAKOV. Well, if you haven't a thousand, then a hundred.

BOBCHINSKY [fumbling in his pockets]. Have you a hundred rubles, Piotr Ivanovich? All I have is forty.

DOBCHINSKY [examining his pocket-book]. I have only twenty-five.

BOBCHINSKY. Look harder, Piotr Ivanovich. I know you have a hole in your pocket, and the money must have dropped down into it somehow.

DOBCHINSKY. No, honestly, there isn't any in the hole either.

KHLESTAKOV. Well, never mind. I merely mentioned the matter. Sixty-five will do. [Takes the money.]

DOBCHINSKY. May I venture to ask a favor of you concerning a very delicate matter?

KHLESTAKOV. What is it?

DOBCHINSKY. It's a matter of an extremely delicate nature. My oldest son--I beg to inform you--was born before I was married.

KHLESTAKOV. Indeed?

DOBCHINSKY. That is, only in a sort of way. He is really my son, just as if he had been born in wedlock. I made up everything afterwards, set everything right, as it should be, with the bonds of matrimony, you know. Now, I venture to inform you, I should like to have him altogether--that is,

I should like him to be altogether my legitimate son and be called Dobchinsky the same as I.

KHLESTAKOV. That's all right. Let him be called Dobchinsky. That's possible.

DOBCHINSKY. I shouldn't have troubled you; but it's a pity, he is such a talented youngster. He gives the greatest promise. He can recite different poems by heart; and whenever he gets hold of a penknife, he makes little carriages as skilfully as a conjurer. Here's Piotr Ivanovich. He knows. Am I not right?

BOBCHINSKY. Yes, the lad is very talented.

KHLESTAKOV. All right, all right. I'll try to do it for you. I'll speak to--I hope--it'll be done, it'll all be done. Yes, yes. [Turning to Bobchinsky.] Have you anything you'd like to say to me?

BOBCHINSKY. Why, of course. I have a most humble request to make.

KHLESTAKOV. What is it?

BOBCHINSKY. I beg your Highness or your Excellency most worshipfully, when you get back to St. Petersburg, please tell all the high personages there, the senators and the admirals, that Piotr Ivanovich Bobchinsky lives in this town. Say this: "Piotr Ivanovich lives there."

KHLESTAKOV. Very well.

BOBCHINSKY. And if you should happen to speak to the Czar, then tell him, too: "Your Majesty," tell him, "Your Majesty, Piotr Ivanovich Bobchinsky lives in this town."

KHLESTAKOV. Very well.

BOBCHINSKY. Pardon me for having troubled you with my presence.

KHLESTAKOV. Not at all, not at all. It was my pleasure. [Sees them to the door.]

SCENE VIII

KHLESTAKOV [alone]. My, there are a lot of officials here. They seem to be taking me for a government functionary. To be sure, I threw dust in their eyes yesterday. What a bunch of fools! I'll write all about it to Triapichkin in St. Petersburg. He'll write them up in the papers. Let him give them a nice walloping.-- Ho, Osip, give me paper and ink.

OSIP [looking in at the door]. D'rectly.

KHLESTAKOV. Anybody gets caught in Triapichkin's tongue had better look out. For the sake of a witticism he wouldn't spare his own father. They are good people though, these officials. It's a nice trait of theirs to lend me money. I'll just see how much it all mounts up to. Here's three hundred from the Judge and three hundred from the Postmaster--six hundred, seven hundred, eight hundred-- What a greasy bill!-- Eight hundred, nine hundred.--Oho! Rolls up to more than a thousand! Now, if I get you, captain, now! We'll see who'll do whom!

SCENE IX

Khlestakov and Osip entering with paper and ink.

KHLESTAKOV. Now, you simpleton, you see how they receive and treat me. [Begins to write.]

OSIP. Yes, thank God! But do you know what, Ivan Aleksandrovich?

KHLESTAKOV. What?

OSIP. Leave this place. Upon my word, it's time.

KHLESTAKOV [writing]. What nonsense! Why?

OSIP. Just so. God be with them. You've had a good time here for two days. It's enough. What's the use of having anything more to do with them? Spit on them. You don't know what may happen. Somebody else may turn up. Upon my word, Ivan Aleksandrovich. And the horses here are fine. We'll gallop away like a breeze.

KHLESTAKOV [writing]. No, I'd like to stay a little longer. Let's go tomorrow.

OSIP. Why tomorrow? Let's go now, Ivan Aleksandrovich, now, 'pon my word. To be sure, it's a great honor and all that. But really we'd better go as quick as we can. You see, they've taken you for somebody else, honest. And your dad will be angry because you dilly-dallied so long. We'd gallop off so smartly. They'd give us first-class horses here.

KHLESTAKOV [writing]. All right. But first take this letter to the postoffice, and, if you like, order post horses at the same time. Tell the postilions that they should drive like couriers and sing songs, and I'll give them a ruble each. [Continues to write.] I wager Triapichkin will die laughing.

OSIP. I'll send the letter off by the man here. I'd rather be packing in the meanwhile so as to lose no time.

KHLESTAKOV. All right. Bring me a candle.

OSIP [outside the door, where he is heard speaking]. Say, partner, go to the post office and mail a letter, and tell the postmaster to frank it. And have a coach sent round at once, the very best courier coach; and tell them the master doesn't pay fare. He travels at the expense of the government. And make them hurry, or else the master will be angry. Wait, the letter isn't ready yet.

KHLESTAKOV. I wonder where he lives now, on Pochtamtskaya or Grokhovaya Street. He likes to move often, too, to get out of paying rent. I'll make a guess and send it to Pochtamtskaya Street. [Folds the letter and addresses it.]

Osip brings the candle. Khlestakov seals the letter with sealing wax. At that moment Derzhimorda's voice is heard saying: "Where are you going, whiskers? You've been told that nobody is allowed to come in."

KHLESTAKOV [giving the letter to Osip]. There, have it mailed.

MERCHANT'S VOICE. Let us in, brother. You have no right to keep us out. We have come on business.

DERZHIMORDA'S VOICE. Get out of here, get out of here! He doesn't receive anybody. He's asleep.

The disturbance outside grows louder.

KHLESTAKOV. What's the matter there, Osip? See what the noise is about.

OSIP [looking through the window]. There are some merchants there who want to come in, and the sergeant won't let them. They are waving papers. I suppose they want to see you.

KHLESTAKOV [going to the window]. What is it, friends?

MERCHANT'S VOICE. We appeal for your protection. Give orders, your Lordship, that our petitions be received.

KHLESTAKOV. Let them in, let them in. Osip, tell them to come in.

Osip goes out.

KHLESTAKOV [takes the petitions through the window, unfolds one of them and reads]. "To his most honorable, illustrious financial Excellency, from the merchant Abdulin. . . ." The devil knows what this is! There's no such title.

SCENE X

Khlestakov and Merchants, with a basket of wine and sugar loaves.

KHLESTAKOV. What is it, friends?

MERCHANTS. We beseech your favor.

KHLESTAKOV. What do you want?

MERCHANTS. Don't ruin us, your Worship. We suffer insult and wrong wholly without cause.

KHLESTAKOV. From whom?

A MERCHANT. Why, from our governor here. Such a governor there never was yet in the world, your Worship. No words can describe the injuries he inflicts upon us. He has taken the bread out of our mouths by quartering soldiers on us, so that you might as well put your neck in a noose. He doesn't treat you as you deserve. He catches hold of your beard and says, "Oh, you Tartar!" Upon my word, if we had shown him any disrespect, but we obey all the laws and regulations. We don't mind giving him what his wife and daughter need for their clothes, but no, that's not enough. So help me God! He comes to our shop and takes whatever his eyes fall on. He sees a piece of cloth and says, "Oh, my friends, that's a fine piece of goods. Take it to my house." So we take it to his house. It will be almost forty yards.

KHLESTAKOV. Is it possible? My, what a swindler!

MERCHANTS. So help us God! No one remembers a governor like him. When you see him coming you hide everything in the shop. It isn't only that he wants a few delicacies and fineries. He takes every bit of trash, too--prunes that have been in the barrel seven years and that even the boy in my shop would not eat, and he grabs a fist full. His name day is St. Anthony's, and you'd think there's nothing else left in the world to bring him and that he doesn't want any more. But no, you must give him more. He says St. Onufry's is also his name day. What's to be done? You have to take things to him on St. Onufry's day, too.

KHLESTAKOV. Why, he's a plain robber.

MERCHANTS. Yes, indeed! And try to contradict him, and he'll fill your house with a whole regiment of soldiers. And if you say anything, he orders the doors closed. "I won't inflict corporal punishment on you," he says, "or put you in the rack. That's forbidden by law," he says. "But I'll make you swallow salt herring, my good man."

KHLESTAKOV. What a swindler! For such things a man can be sent to Siberia.

MERCHANTS. It doesn't matter where you are pleased to send him. Only the farthest away from here the better. Father, don't scorn to accept our bread and salt. We pay our respects to you with sugar and a basket of wine.

KHLESTAKOV. No, no. Don't think of it. I don't take bribes. Oh, if, for example, you would offer me a loan of three hundred rubles, that's quite different. I am willing to take a loan.

MERCHANTS. If you please, father. [They take out money.] But what is three hundred? Better take five hundred. Only help us.

KHLESTAKOV. Very well. About a loan I won't say a word. I'll take it.

MERCHANTS [proffering him the money on a silver tray]. Do please take the tray, too.

KHLESTAKOV. Very well. I can take the tray, too.

MERCHANTS [bowing]. Then take the sugar at the same time.

KHLESTAKOV. Oh, no. I take no bribes.

OSIP. Why don't you take the sugar, your Highness? Take it. Everything will come in handy on the road. Give here the sugar and that case. Give them here. It'll all be of use. What have you got there--a string? Give it here. A string will be handy on the road, too, if the coach or something else should break--for tying it up.

MERCHANTS. Do us this great favor, your illustrious Highness. Why, if you don't help us in our appeal to you, then we simply don't know how we are to exist. We might as well put our necks in a noose.

KHLESTAKOV. Positively, positively. I shall exert my efforts in your behalf.

[The Merchants leave. A woman's voice is heard saying:]

"Don't you dare not to let me in. I'll make a complaint against you to him himself. Don't push me that way. It hurts."

KHLESTAKOV. Who is there? [Goes to the window.] What is it, mother?

[Two women's voices are heard:] "We beseech your grace, father. Give orders, your Lordship, for us to be heard."

KHLESTAKOV. Let her in.

SCENE XI

Khlestakov, the Locksmith's Wife, and the non-commissioned Officer's Widow.

LOCK.'S WIFE [kneeling]. I beseech your grace.

WIDOW. I beseech your grace.

KHLESTAKOV. Who are you?

WIDOW. Ivanova, widow of a non-commissioned officer.

LOCK.'S WIFE. Fevronya Petrova Poshliopkina, the wife of a locksmith, a burgess of this town. My father--

KHLESTAKOV. Stop! One at a time. What do you want?

LOCK.'S WIFE. I beg for your grace. I beseech your aid against the governor. May God send all evil upon him. May neither he nor his children nor his uncles nor his aunts ever prosper in any of their undertakings.

KHLESTAKOV. What's the matter?

LOCK.'S WIFE. He ordered my husband to shave his forehead as a soldier, and our turn hadn't come, and it is against the law, my husband being a married man.

KHLESTAKOV. How could he do it, then?

LOCK.'S WIFE. He did it, he did it, the blackguard! May God smite him both in this world and the next. If he has an aunt, may all harm descend upon her. And if his father is living, may the rascal perish, may he choke to death. Such a cheat! The son of the tailor should have been levied. And he is a drunkard, too. But his parents gave the governor a rich present, so he fastened on the son of the tradeswoman, Panteleyeva. And Panteleyeva also sent his wife three pieces of linen. So then he comes to me. "What do you want your husband for?" he says. "He isn't any good to you any more." It's for me to know whether he is any good or not. That's my business. The old cheat! "He's a thief," he says. "Although he hasn't stolen anything, that doesn't matter. He is going to steal. And he'll be recruited next year anyway." How can I do without a husband? I am not a strong woman. The skunk! May none of his kith and kin ever see the light of God. And if he has a mother-in-law, may she, too,--

KHLESTAKOV. All right, all right. Well, and you?

[Addressing the Widow and leading the Locksmith's Wife to the door.]

LOCK.'S WIFE [leaving]. Don't forget, father. Be kind and gracious to me.

WIDOW. I have come to complain against the Governor, father.

KHLESTAKOV. What is it? What for? Be brief.

WIDOW. He flogged me, father.

KHLESTAKOV. How so?

WIDOW. By mistake, my father. Our women got into a squabble in the market, and when the police came, it was all over, and they took me and reported me-- I couldn't sit down for two days.

KHLESTAKOV. But what's to be done now?

WIDOW. There's nothing to be done, of course. But if you please, order him to pay a fine for the mistake. I can't undo my luck. But the money would be very useful to me now.

KHLESTAKOV. All right, all right. Go now, go. I'll see to it. [Hands with petitions are thrust through the window.] Who else is out there? [Goes to the window.] No, no. I don't want to, I don't want to. [Leaves the window.] I'm sick of it, the devil take it! Don't let them in, Osip.

OSIP [calling through the window]. Go away, go away! He has no time. Come tomorrow.

The door opens and a figure appears in a shag cloak, with unshaven beard, swollen lip, and a bandage over his cheek. Behind him appear a whole line of others.

OSIP. Go away, go away! What are you crowding in here for?

He puts his hands against the stomach of the first one, and goes out through the door, pushing him and banging the door behind.

SCENE XII

Khlestakov and Marya Antonovna.

MARYA. Oh!

KHLESTAKOV. What frightened you so, mademoiselle?

MARYA. I wasn't frightened.

KHLESTAKOV [showing off]. Please, miss. It's a great pleasure to me that you took me for a man who-- May I venture to ask you where you were going?

MARYA. I really wasn't going anywhere.

KHLESTAKOV. But why weren't you going anywhere?

MARYA. I was wondering whether mamma was here.

KHLESTAKOV. No. I'd like to know why you weren't going anywhere.

MARYA. I should have been in your way. You were occupied with important matters.

KHLESTAKOV [showing off]. Your eyes are better than important matters. You cannot possibly disturb me. No, indeed, by no means. On the contrary, you afford me great pleasure.

MARYA. You speak like a man from the capital.

KHLESTAKOV. For such a beautiful lady as you. May I give myself the pleasure of offering you a chair? But no, you should have, not a chair, but a throne.

MARYA. I really don't know--I really must go [She sits down.]

KHLESTAKOV. What a beautiful scarf that is.

MARYA. You are making fun of me. You're only ridiculing the provincials.

KHLESTAKOV. Oh, mademoiselle, how I long to be your scarf, so that I might embrace your lily neck.

MARYA. I haven't the least idea what you are talking about--scarf!--Peculiar weather today, isn't it?

KHLESTAKOV. Your lips, mademoiselle, are better than any weather.

MARYA. You are just saying that--I should like to ask you--I'd rather you would write some verses in my album for a souvenir. You must know very many.

KHLESTAKOV. Anything you desire, mademoiselle. Ask! What verses will you have?

MARYA. Any at all. Pretty, new verses.

KHLESTAKOV. Oh, what are verses! I know a lot of them.

MARYA. Well, tell me. What verses will you write for me?

KHLESTAKOV. What's the use? I know them anyway.

MARYA. I love them so.

KHLESTAKOV. I have lots of them--of every sort. If you like, for example, I'll give you this: "Oh, thou, mortal man, who in thy anguish murmurest against God--" and others. I can't remember them now. Besides, it's all bosh. I'd rather offer you my love instead, which ever since your first glance-- [Moves his chair nearer.]

MARYA. Love? I don't understand love. I never knew what love is. [Moves her chair away.]

KHLESTAKOV. Why do you move your chair away? It is better for us to sit near each other.

MARYA [moving away]. Why near? It's all the same if it's far away.

KHLESTAKOV [moving nearer]. Why far? It's all the same if it's near.

MARYA [moving away]. But what for?

KHLESTAKOV [moving nearer]. It only seems near to you. Imagine it's far. How happy I would be, mademoiselle, if I could clasp you in my embrace.

MARYA [looking through the window]. What is that? It looked as if something had flown by. Was it a magpie or some other bird?

KHLESTAKOV [kisses her shoulder and looks through the window]. It's a magpie.

MARYA [rises indignantly]. No, that's too much-- Such rudeness, such impertinence.

KHLESTAKOV [holding her back]. Forgive me, mademoiselle. I did it only out of love--only out of love, nothing else.

MARYA. You take me for a silly provincial wench. [Struggles to go away.]

KHLESTAKOV [still holding her back]. It's out of love, really--out of love. It was just a little fun. Marya Antonovna, don't be angry. I'm ready to beg your forgiveness on my knees. [Falls on his knees.] Forgive me, do forgive me! You see, I am on my knees.

SCENE XIII

The same and Anna Andreyevna.

ANNA [seeing Khlestakov on his knees]. Oh, what a situation!

KHLESTAKOV [rising]. Oh, the devil!

ANNA [to Marya]. What does this mean? What does this behavior mean?

MARYA. I, mother--

ANNA. Go away from here. Do you hear? And don't you dare to show your face to me. [Marya goes out in tears.] Excuse me. I must say I'm greatly astonished.

KHLESTAKOV [aside]. She's very appetizing, too. She's not bad-looking, either. [Flings himself on his knees.] Madam, you see I am burning with love.

ANNA. What! You on your knees? Please get up, please get up. This floor isn't very clean.

KHLESTAKOV. No, I must be on my knees before you. I must. Pronounce the verdict. Is it life or death?

ANNA. But please--I don't quite understand the significance of your words. If I am not mistaken, you are making a proposal for my daughter.

KHLESTAKOV. No, I am in love with you. My life hangs by a thread. If you don't crown my steadfast love, then I am not fit to exist in this world. With a burning flame in my bosom, I pray for your hand.

ANNA. But please remember I am in a certain way --married.

KHLESTAKOV. That's nothing. Love knows no distinction. It was Karamzin who said: "The laws condemn." We will fly in the shadow of a brook. Your hand! I pray for your hand!

SCENE XIV

The same and Marya Antonovna.

MARYA [running in suddenly]. Mamma, papa says you should--[seeing Khlestakov on his knees, exclaims:] Oh, what a situation!

ANNA. Well, what do you want? Why did you come in here? What for? What sort of flightiness is this? Breaks in like a cat leaping out of smoke. Well, what have you found so wonderful? What's gotten into your head again? Really, she behaves like a child of three. She doesn't act a bit like a girl of eighteen, not a bit. I don't know when you'll get more sense into your head, when you'll behave like a decent, well-bred girl, when you'll know what good manners are and a proper demeanor.

MARYA [through her tears]. Mamma, I really didn't know--

ANNA. There's always a breeze blowing through your head. You act like Liapkin-Tiapkin's daughter. Why should you imitate them? You shouldn't imitate them. You have other examples to follow. You have your mother before you. She's the example to follow.

KHLESTAKOV [seizing Marya's hand]. Anna Andreyevna, don't oppose our happiness. Give your blessing to our constant love.

ANNA [in surprise]. So it's in her you are--

KHLESTAKOV. Decide--life or death?

ANNA. Well, there, you fool, you see? Our guest is pleased to go down on his knees for such trash as you. You, running in suddenly as if you were out of your mind. Really, it would be just what you deserve, if I refused. You are not worthy of such happiness.

MARYA. I won't do it again, mamma, really I won't.

SCENE XV

The same and the Governor in precipitate haste.

GOVERNOR. Your Excellency, don't ruin me, don't ruin me.

KHLESTAKOV. What's the matter?

GOVERNOR. The merchants have complained to your Excellency. I assure you on my honor that not one half of what they said is so. They themselves are cheats. They give short measure and short weight. The officer's widow lied to you when she said I flogged her. She lied, upon my word, she lied. She flogged herself.

KHLESTAKOV. The devil take the officer's widow. What do I care about the officer's widow.

GOVERNOR. Don't believe them, don't believe them. They are rank liars; a mere child wouldn't believe them. They are known all over town as liars. And as for cheating, I venture to inform you that there are no swindlers like them in the whole of creation.

ANNA. Do you know what honor Ivan Aleksandrovich is bestowing upon us? He is asking for our daughter's hand.

GOVERNOR. What are you talking about? Mother has lost her wits. Please do not be angry, your Excellency. She has a touch of insanity. Her mother was like that, too.

KHLESTAKOV. Yes, I am really asking for your daughter's hand. I am in love with her.

GOVERNOR. I cannot believe it, your Excellency.

ANNA. But when you are told!

KHLESTAKOV. I am not joking. I could go crazy, I am so in love.

GOVERNOR. I daren't believe it. I am unworthy of such an honor.

KHLESTAKOV. If you don't consent to give me your daughter Marya Antonovna's hand, then I am ready to do the devil knows what.

GOVERNOR. I cannot believe it. You deign to joke, your Excellency.

ANNA. My, what a blockhead! Really! When you are told over and over again!

GOVERNOR. I can't believe it.

KHLESTAKOV. Give her to me, give her to me! I am a desperate man and I may do anything. If I shoot myself, you will have a law-suit on your hands.

GOVERNOR. Oh, my God! I am not guilty either in thought or in action. Please do not be angry. Be pleased to act as your mercy wills. Really, my head is in such a state I don't know what is happening. I have turned into a worse fool than I've ever been in my life.

ANNA. Well, give your blessing.

Khlestakov goes up to Marya Antonovna.

GOVERNOR. May God bless you, but I am not guilty. [Khlestakov kisses Marya. The Governor looks at them.] What the devil! It's really so. [Rubs his eyes.] They are kissing. Oh, heavens! They are kissing. Actually to be our son-in-law! [Cries out, jumping with glee.] Ho, Anton! Ho, Anton! Ho, Governor! So that's the turn events have taken!

SCENE XVI

The same and Osip.

OSIP. The horses are ready.

KHLESTAKOV. Oh! All right. I'll come presently.

GOVERNOR. What's that? Are you leaving?

KHLESTAKOV. Yes, I'm going.

GOVERNOR. Then when--that is--I thought you were pleased to hint at a wedding.

KHLESTAKOV. Oh--for one minute only--for one day--to my uncle, a rich old man. I'll be back tomorrow.

GOVERNOR. We would not venture, of course, to hold you back, and we hope for your safe return.

KHLESTAKOV. Of course, of course, I'll come back at once. Good-by, my dear--no, I simply can't express my feelings. Good-by, my heart. [Kisses Marya's hand.]

GOVERNOR. Don't you need something for the road? It seems to me you were pleased to be short of cash.

KHLESTAKOV, Oh, no, what for? [After a little thought.] However, if you like.

GOVERNOR. How much will you have?

KHLESTAKOV. You gave me two hundred then, that is, not two hundred, but four hundred--I don't want to take advantage of your mistake--you might let me have the same now so that it should be an even eight hundred.

GOVERNOR. Very well. [Takes the money out of his pocket-book.] The notes happen to be brand-new, too, as though on purpose.

KHLESTAKOV. Oh, yes. [Takes the bills and looks at them.] That's good. They say new money means good luck.

GOVERNOR. Quite right.

KHLESTAKOV. Good-by, Anton Antonovich. I am very much obliged to you for your hospitality. I admit with all my heart that I have never got such a good reception anywhere. Good-by, Anna Andreyevna. Good-by, my sweet-heart, Marya Antonovna.

All go out.

Behind the Scenes.

KHLESTAKOV. Good-by, angel of my soul, Marya Antonovna.

GOVERNOR. What's that? You are going in a plain mail-coach?

KHLESTAKOV. Yes, I'm used to it. I get a headache from a carriage with springs.

POSTILION. Ho!

GOVERNOR. Take a rug for the seat at least. If you say so, I'll tell them to bring a rug.

KHLESTAKOV. No, what for? It's not necessary. However, let them bring a rug if you please.

GOVERNOR. Ho, Avdotya. Go to the store-room and bring the very best rug from there, the Persian rug with the blue ground. Quick!

POSTILION. Ho!

GOVERNOR. When do you say we are to expect you back?

KHLESTAKOV. Tomorrow, or the day after.

OSIP. Is this the rug? Give it here. Put it there. Now put some hay on this side.

POSTILION. Ho!

OSIP. Here, on this side. More. All right. That will be fine. [Beats the rug down with his hand.] Now take the seat, your Excellency.

KHLESTAKOV. Good-by, Anton Antonovich.

GOVERNOR. Good-by, your Excellency.

ANNA } MARYA} Good-by, Ivan Aleksandrovich.

KHLESTAKOV. Good-by, mother.

POSTILION. Get up, my boys!

The bell rings and the curtain drops.

ACT V

SCENE: Same as in Act IV.

SCENE I

Governor, Anna Andreyevna, and Marya Antonovna.

GOVERNOR. Well, Anna Andreyevna, eh? Did you ever imagine such a thing? Such a rich prize? I'll be--. Well, confess frankly, it never occurred to you even in your dreams, did it? From just a simple governor's wife suddenly--whew!--I'll be hanged! --to marry into the family of such a big gun.

ANNA. Not at all. I knew it long ago. It seems wonderful to you because you are so plain. You never saw decent people.

GOVERNOR. I'm a decent person myself, mother. But, really, think, Anna Andreyevna, what gay birds we have turned into now, you and I. Eh, Anna Andreyevna? High fliers, by Jove! Wait now, I'll give those fellows who were so eager to present their petitions and denunciations a peppering. Ho, who's there? [Enter a Sergeant.] Is it you, Ivan Karpovich? Call those merchants here, brother, won't you? I'll give it to them, the scoundrels! To make such complaints against me! The damned pack of Jews! Wait, my dear fellows. I used to dose you down to your ears. Now I'll dose you down to your beards. Make a list of all who came to protest against me, especially the mean petty scribblers who cooked the petitions up for them, and announce to all that they should know what honor the Heavens have bestowed upon the Governor, namely this: that he is marrying his daughter, not to a plain ordinary man, but to one the like of whom has never yet been in the world, who can do everything, everything, everything, everything! Proclaim it to all so that everybody should know. Shout it aloud to the whole world. Ring the bell, the devil take it! It is a triumph, and we will make it a triumph. [The Sergeant goes out.] So that's the way, Anna Andreyevna, eh? What shall we do now? Where shall we live? Here or in St. Pete?

ANNA. In St. Petersburg, of course. How could we remain here?

GOVERNOR. Well, if St. Pete, then St. Pete. But it would be good here, too. I suppose the governorship could then go to the devil, eh, Anna Andreyevna?

ANNA. Of course. What's a governorship?

GOVERNOR. Don't you think, Anna Andreyevna, I can rise to a high rank now, he being hand in glove with all the ministers, and visiting the court? In time I can be promoted to a generalship. What do you think, Anna Andreyevna? Can I become a general?

ANNA. I should say so. Of course you can.

GOVERNOR. Ah, the devil take it, it's nice to be a general. They hang a ribbon across your shoulders. What ribbon is better, the red St. Anne or the blue St. Andrew?

ANNA. The blue St. Andrew, of course.

GOVERNOR. What! My, you're aiming high. The red one is good, too. Why does one want to be a general? Because when you go travelling, there are always couriers and aides on ahead with "Horses"! And at the stations they refuse to give the horses to others. They all wait, all those councilors, captains, governors, and you don't take the slightest notice of them. You dine somewhere with the governor-general. And the town-governor--I'll keep him waiting at the door. Ha, ha, ha! [He bursts into a roar of laughter, shaking all over.] That's what's so alluring, confound it!

ANNA. You always like such coarse things. You must remember that our life will have to be completely changed, that your acquaintances will not be a dog-lover of a judge, with whom you go hunting hares, or a Zemlianika. On the contrary, your acquaintances will be people of the most refined type, counts, and society aristocrats. Only really I am afraid of you. You sometimes use words that one never hears in good society.

GOVERNOR. What of it? A word doesn't hurt.

ANNA. It's all right when you are a town-governor, but there the life is entirely different.

GOVERNOR. Yes, they say there are two kinds of fish there, the sea-eel and the smelt, and before you start to eat them, the saliva flows in your mouth.

ANNA. That's all he thinks about--fish. I shall insist upon our house being the first in the capital and my room having so much amber in it that when you come in you have to shut your eyes. [She shuts her eyes and sniffs.] Oh, how good!

SCENE II

The same and the Merchants.

GOVERNOR. Ah, how do you do, my fine fellows?

MERCHANTS [bowing]. We wish you health, father.

GOVERNOR. Well, my dearly beloved friends, how are you? How are your goods selling? So you complained against me, did you, you tea tanks, you scurvy hucksters? Complain, against me? You crooks, you pirates, you. Did you gain a lot by it, eh? Aha, you thought you'd land me in prison? May seven devils and one she-devil take you! Do you know that--

ANNA. Good heavens, Antosha, what words you use!

GOVERNOR [irritated]. Oh, it isn't a matter of words now. Do you know that the very official to whom you complained is going to marry my daughter? Well, what do you say to that? Now I'll make you smart. You cheat the people, you make a contract with the government, and you do the government out of a hundred thousand, supplying it with rotten cloth; and when you give fifteen yards away gratis, you expect a reward besides. If they knew, they would send you to-- And you strut about sticking out your paunches with a great air of importance: "I'm a merchant, don't touch me." "We," you say, "are as good as the nobility." Yes, the nobility, you monkey-faces. The nobleman is educated. If he gets flogged in school, it is for a purpose, to learn something useful. And you--start out in life learning trickery. Your master beats you for not being able to cheat. When you are still little boys and don't know the Lord's Prayer, you already give short measure and short weight. And when your bellies swell and your pockets fill up, then you assume an air of importance. Whew! What marvels! Because you guzzle sixteen samovars full a day, that's why you put on an air of importance. I spit on your heads and on your importance.

MERCHANTS [bowing]. We are guilty, Anton Antonovich.

GOVERNOR. Complaining, eh? And who helped you with that grafting when you built a bridge and charged twenty thousand for wood when there wasn't even a hundred rubles' worth used? I did. You goat beards. Have you forgotten? If I had informed on you, I could have despatched you to Siberia. What do you say to that?

A MERCHANT. I'm guilty before God, Anton Antonovich. The evil spirit tempted me. We will never complain against you again. Ask whatever satisfaction you want, only don't be angry.

GOVERNOR. Don't be angry! Now you are crawling at my feet. Why? Because I am on top now. But if the balance dipped the least bit your way, then you would trample me in the very dirt--you scoundrels! And you would crush me under a beam besides.

MERCHANTS [prostrating themselves]. Don't ruin us, Anton Antonovich.

GOVERNOR. Don't ruin us! Now you say, don't ruin us! And what did you say before? I could give you--[shrugging his shoulders and throwing up his hands.] Well, God forgive you. Enough. I don't harbor malice for long. Only look out now. Be on your guard. My daughter is going to marry, not an ordinary nobleman. Let your congratulations be-- you understand?

Don't try to get away with a dried sturgeon or a loaf of sugar. Well, leave now, in God's name.

Merchants leave.

SCENE III

The same, Ammos Fiodorovich, Artemy Filippovich, then Rastakovsky.

AMMOS [in the doorway]. Are we to believe the report, Anton Antonovich? A most extraordinary piece of good fortune has befallen you, hasn't it?

ARTEMY. I have the honor to congratulate you on your unusual good fortune. I was glad from the bottom of my heart when I heard it. [Kisses Anna's hand.] Anna Andreyevna! [Kissing Marya's hand.] Marya Antonovna!

Rastakovsky enters.

RASTAKOVSKY. I congratulate you, Anton Antonovich. May God give you and the new couple long life and may He grant you numerous progeny--grand-children and great-grand-children. Anna Andreyevna! [Kissing her hand.] Marya Antonovna! [Kissing her hand.]

SCENE IV

The same, Korobkin and his Wife, Liuliukov.

KOROBKIN. I have the honor to congratulate you, Anton Antonovich, and you, Anna Andreyevna [kissing her hand] and you Marya Antonovna [kissing her hand].

KOROBKIN'S WIFE. I congratulate you from the bottom of my heart, Anna Andreyevna, on your new stroke of good fortune.

LIULIUKOV. I have the honor to congratulate you, Anna Andreyevna. [Kisses her hand and turns to the audience, smacks his lips, putting on a bold front.] Marya Antonovna, I have the honor to congratulate you. [Kisses her hand and turns to the audience in the same way.]

SCENE V

A number of Guests enter. They kiss Anna's hand saying: "Anna Andreyevna," then Marya's hand, saying "Marya Antonovna."

Bobchinsky and Dobchinsky enter jostling each other.

BOBCHINSKY. I have the honor to congratulate you.

DOBCHINSKY. Anton Antonovich, I have the honor to congratulate you.

BOBCHINSKY. On the happy event.

DOBCHINSKY. Anna Andreyevna!

BOBCHINSKY. Anna Andreyevna!

They bend over her hand at the same time and bump foreheads.

DOBCHINSKY. Marya Antonovna! [Kisses her hand.] I have the honor to congratulate you. You will enjoy the greatest happiness. You will wear garments of gold and eat the most delicate soups, and you will pass your time most entertainingly.

BOBCHINSKY [breaking in]. God give you all sorts of riches and of money and a wee tiny little son, like this. [Shows the size with his hands.] So that he can sit on the palm of your hand. The little fellow will be crying all the time, "Wow, wow, wow."

SCENE VI

More Guests enter and kiss the ladies' hands, among them Luka Lukich and his wife.

LUKA LUKICH. I have the honor.

LUKA'S WIFE [running ahead]. Congratulate you, Anna Andreyevna. [They kiss.] Really, I was so glad to hear of it. They tell me, "Anna Andreyevna has betrothed her daughter." "Oh, my God," I think to myself. It made me so glad that I said to my husband, "Listen, Lukanchik, that's a great piece of fortune for Anna Andreyevna." "Well," think I to myself, "thank God!" And I say to him, "I'm so delighted that I'm consumed with impatience to tell it to Anna Andreyevna herself." "Oh, my God," think I to myself, "it's just as Anna Andreyevna expected. She always did expect a good match for her daughter. And now what luck! It happened just exactly as she wanted it to happen." Really, it made me so glad that I couldn't say a word. I cried and cried. I simply screamed, so that Luka Lukich said to me, "What are you crying so for, Nastenka?" "Lukanchik," I said, "I don't know myself. The tears just keep flowing like a stream."

GOVERNOR. Please sit down, ladies and gentlemen. Ho, Mishka, bring some more chairs in.

The Guests seat themselves.

SCENE VII

The same, the Police Captain and Sergeants.

CAPTAIN. I have the honor to congratulate you, your Honor, and to wish you long years of prosperity.

GOVERNOR. Thank you, thank you! Please sit down, gentlemen.

The Guests seat themselves.

AMMOS. But please tell us, Anton Antonovich, how did it all come about, and how did it all--ahem!-- go?

GOVERNOR. It went in a most extraordinary way. He condescended to make the proposal in his own person.

ANNA. In the most respectful and most delicate manner. He spoke beautifully. He said: "Anna Andreyevna, I have only a feeling of respect for your worth." And such a handsome, cultured man! His manners so genteel! "Believe me, Anna Andreyevna," he says, "life is not worth a penny to me. It is only because I respect your rare qualities."

MARYA. Oh, mamma, it was to me he said that.

ANNA. Shut up! You don't know anything. And don't meddle in other people's affairs. "Anna Andreyevna," he says, "I am enraptured." That was the flattering way he poured out his soul. And when I was going to say,

"We cannot possibly hope for such an honor," he suddenly went down on his knees, and so aristocratically! "Anna Andreyevna," he says, "don't make me the most miserable of men. Consent to respond to my feelings, or else I'll put an end to my life."

MARYA. Really, mamma, it was to me he said that.

ANNA. Yes, of course--to you, too. I don't deny it.

GOVERNOR. He even frightened us. He said he would put a bullet through his brains. "I'll shoot myself, I'll shoot myself," he said.

MANY GUESTS. Well, for the Lord's sake!

AMMOS. How remarkable!

LUKA. It must have been fate that so ordained.

ARTEMY. Not fate, my dear friend. Fate is a turkey-hen. It was the Governor's services that brought him this piece of fortune. [Aside.] Good luck always does crawl into the mouths of swine like him.

AMMOS. If you like, Anton Antonovich, I'll sell you the dog we were bargaining about.

GOVERNOR. I don't care about dogs now.

AMMOS. Well, if you don't want it, then we'll agree on some other dog.

KOROBKIN'S WIFE. Oh, Anna Andreyevna, how happy I am over your good fortune. You can't imagine how happy I am.

KOROBKIN. But where, may I ask, is the distinguished guest now? I heard he had gone away for some reason or other.

GOVERNOR. Yes, he's gone off for a day on a highly important matter.

ANNA. To his uncle--to ask his blessing.

GOVERNOR. To ask his blessing. But tomorrow-- [He sneezes, and all burst into one exclamation of well-wishes.] Thank you very much. But tomorrow he'll be back. [He sneezes, and is congratulated again. Above the other voices are heard those of the following.]

{CAPTAIN. I wish you health, your Honor.

{BOBCHINSKY. A hundred years and a sack of ducats.

{DOBCHINSKY. May God increase it to a thousand.

{ARTEMY. May you go to hell!

{KOROBKIN'S WIFE. The devil take you!

GOVERNOR. I'm very much obliged to you. I wish you the same.

ANNA. We intend to live in St. Petersburg now. I must say, the atmosphere here is too village-like. I must say, it's extremely unpleasant. My husband, too --he'll be made a general there.

GOVERNOR. Yes, confound it, gentlemen, I admit I should very much like to be a general.

LUKA. May God grant that you get a generalship.

RASTAKOVSKY. From man it is impossible, but from God everything is possible.

AMMOS. High merits, high honors.

ARTEMY. Reward according to service.

AMMOS [aside]. The things he'll do when he becomes a general. A generalship suits him as a saddle suits a cow. It's a far cry to his generalship. There are better men than you, and they haven't been made generals yet.

ARTEMY [aside]. The devil take it--he's aiming for a generalship. Well, maybe he will become a general after all. He's got the air of importance, the devil take him! [Addressing the Governor.] Don't forget us then, Anton Antonovich.

AMMOS. And if anything happens--for instance, some difficulty in our affairs--don't refuse us your protection.

KOROBKIN. Next year I am going to take my son to the capital to put him in government service. So do me the kindness to give me your protection. Be a father to the orphan.

GOVERNOR. I am ready for my part--ready to exert my efforts on your behalf.

ANNA. Antosha, you are always ready with your promises. In the first place, you won't have time to think of such things. And how can you--how is it possible for you, to burden yourself with such promises?

GOVERNOR. Why not, my dear? It's possible occasionally.

ANNA. Of course it's possible. But you can't give protection to every small potato.

KOROBKIN'S WIFE. Do you hear the way she speaks of us?

GUEST. She's always been that way. I know her. Seat her at table and she'll put her feet on it.

SCENE VIII

The same and the Postmaster, who rushes in with an unsealed letter in his hand.

POSTMASTER. A most astonishing thing, ladies and gentlemen! The official whom we took to be an inspector-general is not an inspector-general.

ALL. How so? Not an inspector-general?

POSTMASTER. No, not a bit of it. I found it out from the letter.

GOVERNOR. What are you talking about? What are you talking about? What letter?

POSTMASTER. His own letter. They bring a letter to the postoffice, I glance at the address and I see Pochtamtskaya Street. I was struck dumb.

"Well," I think to myself, "I suppose he found something wrong in the postoffice department and is informing the government." So I unsealed it.

GOVERNOR. How could you?

POSTMASTER. I don't know myself. A supernatural power moved me. I had already summoned a courier to send it off by express; but I was overcome by a greater curiosity than I have ever felt in my life. "I can't, I can't," I hear a voice telling me. "I can't." But it pulled me and pulled me. In one ear I heard, "Don't open the letter. You will die like a chicken," and in the other it was just as if the devil were whispering, "Open it, open it." And when I cracked the sealing wax, I felt as if I were on fire; and when I opened the letter, I froze, upon my word, I froze. And my hands trembled, and everything whirled around me.

GOVERNOR. But how did you dare to open it? The letter of so powerful a personage?

POSTMASTER. But that's just the point--he's neither powerful nor a personage.

GOVERNOR. Then what is he in your opinion?

POSTMASTER. He's neither one thing nor another. The devil knows what he is.

GOVERNOR [furiously]. How neither one thing nor another? How do you dare to call him neither one thing nor another? And the devil knows what besides? I'll put you under arrest.

POSTMASTER. Who--you?

GOVERNOR. Yes, I.

POSTMASTER. You haven't the power.

GOVERNOR. Do you know that he's going to marry my daughter? That I myself am going to be a high official and will have the power to exile to Siberia?

POSTMASTER. Oh, Anton Antonovich, Siberia! Siberia is far away. I'd rather read the letter to you. Ladies and gentlemen, permit me to read the letter.

ALL. Do read it.

POSTMASTER [reads]. "I hasten to inform you, my dear friend, what wonderful things have happened to me. On the way here an infantry captain did me out of my last penny, so that the innkeeper here wanted to send me to jail, when suddenly, thanks to my St. Petersburg appearance and dress, the whole town took me for a governor-general. Now I am staying at the governor's home. I am having a grand time and I am flirting desperately with his wife and daughter. I only haven't decided whom to begin with. I think with the mother first, because she seems ready to accept all terms. You remember how hard up we were taking our meals wherever we could without paying for them, and how once the pastry cook grabbed me by the collar for having charged pies that I ate to the king of England? Now it is quite different. They lend me all the money I want. They are an awful lot of originals. You would split your sides laughing at them. I know you write for the papers. Put them in your literature. In the first place the Governor is as stupid as an old horse--"

GOVERNOR. Impossible! That can't be in the letter.

POSTMASTER [showing the letter]. Read for yourself.

GOVERNOR [reads]. "As an old horse." Impossible! You put it in yourself.

POSTMASTER. How could I?

ARTEMY. Go on reading.

LUKA. Go on reading.

POSTMASTER [continuing to read]. "The Governor is as stupid as an old horse--"

GOVERNOR. Oh, the devil! He's got to read it again. As if it weren't there anyway.

POSTMASTER [continuing to read]. H'm, h'm--"an old horse. The Postmaster is a good man, too." [Stops reading.] Well, here he's saying something improper about me, too.

GOVERNOR. Go on--read the rest.

POSTMASTER. What for?

GOVERNOR. The deuce take it! Once we have begun to read it, we must read it all.

ARTEMY. If you will allow me, I will read it. [Puts on his eye-glasses and reads.] "The Postmaster is just like the porter Mikheyev in our office, and the scoundrel must drink just as hard."

POSTMASTER [to the audience]. A bad boy! He ought to be given a licking. That's all.

ARTEMY [continues to read]. "The Superintendent of Char-i-i--" [Stammers.]

KOROBKIN. Why did you stop?

ARTEMY. The handwriting isn't clear. Besides, it's evident that he's a blackguard.

KOROBKIN. Give it to me. I believe my eyesight is better.

ARTEMY [refusing to give up the letter]. No. This part can be omitted. After that it's legible.

KOROBKIN. Let me have it please. I'll see for myself.

ARTEMY. I can read it myself. I tell you that after this part it's all legible.

POSTMASTER. No, read it all. Everything so far could be read.

ALL. Give him the letter, Artemy Filippovich, give it to him. [To Korobkin.] You read it.

ARTEMY. Very well. [Gives up the letter.] Here it is. [Covers a part of it with his finger.] Read from here on. [All press him.]

POSTMASTER. Read it all, nonsense, read it all.

KOROBKIN [reading]. "The Superintendent of Charities, Zemlianika, is a regular pig in a cap."

ARTEMY [to the audience]. Not a bit witty. A pig in a cap! Have you ever seen a pig wear a cap?

KOROBKIN [continues reading]. "The School Inspector reeks of onions."

LUKA [to the audience]. Upon my word, I never put an onion to my mouth.

AMMOS [aside]. Thank God, there's nothing about me in it.

KOROBKIN [continues reading]. "The Judge--"

AMMOS. There! [Aloud.] Ladies and gentlemen, I think the letter is far too long. To the devil with it! Why should we go on reading such trash?

LUKA. No.

POSTMASTER. No, go on.

ARTEMY. Go on reading.

KOROBKIN. "The Judge, Liapkin-Tiapkin, is extremely mauvais ton." [He stops.] That must be a French word.

AMMOS. The devil knows what it means. It wouldn't be so bad if all it means is "cheat." But it may mean something worse.

KOROBKIN [continues reading]. "However, the people are hospitable and kindhearted. Farewell, my dear Triapichkin. I want to follow your example and take up literature. It's tiresome to live this way, old boy. One wants food for the mind, after all. I see I must engage in something lofty. Address me: Village of Podkatilovka in the Government of Saratov." [Turns the letter and reads the address.] "Mr. Ivan Vasilyevich Triapichkin, St. Petersburg, Pochtamtskaya Street, House Number 97, Courtyard, third floor, right."

A LADY. What an unexpected rebuke!

GOVERNOR. He has cut my throat and cut it for good. I'm done for, completely done for. I see nothing. All I see are pigs' snouts instead of faces, and nothing more. Catch him, catch him! [Waves his hand.]

POSTMASTER. Catch him! How? As if on purpose, I told the overseer to give him the best coach and three. The devil prompted me to give the order.

KOROBKIN'S WIFE. Here's a pretty mess.

AMMOS. Confound it, he borrowed three hundred rubles from me.

ARTEMY. He borrowed three hundred from me, too.

POSTMASTER [sighing]. And from me, too.

BOBCHINSKY. And sixty-five from me and Piotr Ivanovich.

AMMOS [throwing up his hands in perplexity]. How's that, gentlemen? Really, how could we have been so off our guard?

GOVERNOR [beating his forehead]. How could I, how could I, old fool? I've grown childish, stupid mule. I have been in the service thirty years. Not one merchant, not one contractor has been able to impose on me. I have over-reached one swindler after another. I have caught crooks and sharpers that were ready to rob the whole world. I have fooled three governor-generals. As for governor-generals, [with a wave of his hand] it is not even worth talking about them.

ANNA. But how is it possible, Antosha? He's engaged to Mashenka.

GOVERNOR [in a rage]. Engaged! Rats! Fiddlesticks! So much for your engagement! Thrusts her engagement at me now! [In a frenzy.] Here, look at me! Look at me, the whole world, the whole of Christendom. See what a fool the governor was made of. Out upon him, the fool, the old scoundrel! [Shakes his fist at himself.] Oh, you fat-nose! To take an icicle, a rag for a personage of rank! Now his coach bells are jingling all along the road. He is publishing the story to the whole world. Not only will you be made a laughing-stock of, but some scribbler, some ink-splasher will put you into a comedy. There's the horrid sting. He won't spare either rank or station. And everybody will grin and clap his hands. What are you laughing at?

You are laughing at yourself, oh you! [Stamps his feet.] I would give it to all those ink-splashers! You scribblers, damned liberals, devil's brood! I would tie you all up in a bundle, I would grind you into meal, and give it to the devil. [Shakes his fist and stamps his heel on the floor. After a brief silence.] I can't come to myself. It's really true, whom the gods want to punish they first make mad. In what did that nincompoop resemble an inspector-general? In nothing, not even half the little finger of an inspector-general. And all of a sudden everybody is going about saying, "Inspector-general, inspector-general." Who was the first to say it? Tell me.

ARTEMY [throwing up his hands]. I couldn't tell how it happened if I had to die for it. It is just as if a mist had clouded our brains. The devil has confounded us.

AMMOS. Who was the first to say it? These two here, this noble pair. [Pointing to Dobchinsky and Bobchinsky.]

BOBCHINSKY. So help me God, not I. I didn't even think of it.

DOBCHINSKY. I didn't say a thing, not a thing.

ARTEMY. Of course you did.

LUKA. Certainly. You came running here from the inn like madmen. "He's come, he's come. He doesn't pay." Found a rare bird!

GOVERNOR. Of course it was you. Town gossips, damned liars!

ARTEMY. The devil take you with your inspector-general and your tattle.

GOVERNOR. You run about the city, bother everybody, confounded chatterboxes. You spread gossip, you short-tailed magpies, you!

AMMOS. Damned bunglers!

LUKA. Simpletons.

ARTEMY. Pot-bellied mushrooms!

All crowd around them.

BOBCHINSKY. Upon my word, it wasn't I. It was Piotr Ivanovich.

DOBCHINSKY. No, Piotr Ivanovich, you were the first.

BOBCHINSKY. No, no. You were the first.

LAST SCENE

The same and a Gendarme.

GENDARME. An official from St. Petersburg sent by imperial order has arrived, and wants to see you all at once. He is stopping at the inn.

All are struck as by a thunderbolt. A cry of amazement bursts from the ladies simultaneously. The whole group suddenly shifts positions and remains standing as if petrified.

SILENT SCENE

The Governor stands in the center rigid as a post, with outstretched hands and head thrown backward. On his right are his wife and daughter straining toward him. Back of them the Postmaster, turned toward the audience, metamorphosed into a question mark. Next to him, at the edge of the group, three lady guests leaning on each other, with a most satirical expression on their faces directed straight at the Governor's family. To the left of the Governor is Zemlianika, his head to one side as if listening. Behind him is the Judge with outspread hands almost crouching on the ground and pursing his lips as if to whistle or say: "A nice pickle we're in!" Next to him is Korobkin, turned toward the audience, with eyes screwed up and making a venomous gesture at the Governor. Next to him, at the edge of the group, are Dobchinsky and Bobchinsky, gesticulating at each other, open-mouthed and wide-eyed. The other guests remain standing stiff. The whole group retain the same position of rigidity for almost a minute and a half. The curtain falls.

THE END

Made in the USA
Coppell, TX
24 July 2023